Elon Musk

Futurist: A Biography of Elon's Success, Challenges, and Ambitions with Tesla, SpaceX, Twitter, and Politics

William Isaac

Copyright ©2024. William Isaac

All rights reserved. To protect individual privacy, certain names and identifying details have been changed. The events, settings, and dialogues presented have been recreated based on the author's intensive research. For anonymity, some names, locations, and other identifying characteristics—such as physical features, occupations, and residences—may have been altered.

No part of this publication may be reproduced, stored in any retrieval system, or shared in any form or by any means (whether mechanical, electronic, recording, photocopying, or otherwise) without the express written consent of the copyright holder. Unauthorized use is prohibited and may result in legal consequences.

Table of Contents

Introduction

Early Years: Elon Musk's Formative Years

The Early Career of Elon Musk: A Journey of Vision, Struggle, and Resilience

Later Career: Transforming the World, One Idea at a Time

Present Day: Neuralink, The Boring Company, and X

Present Day: Politics and Family Life

Elon Musk: A Deeper Dive into Political Challenges and Collaborations

The Future

Timeline of Elon Musk's Life

Trivia Questions

Answers to Trivia Questions

Discussion Questions

Introduction

Elon Musk is a name that makes you think of innovative ideas and big goals. Musk has changed everything from electric cars to space travel as the founder of Tesla, SpaceX, Neuralink, and other groundbreaking companies. A limited number of individuals have significantly influenced technology and the destiny of humanity. This biography explores the person behind the initiatives, illustrating how his distinctive experiences have influenced his ideas and how his relentless pursuit of development continues to inspire innovation across the globe.

Topics about Elon will include co-founding of Zip2, PayPal, SpaceX, and Tesla. From his 2008 bankruptcy scare to his ongoing battles with critics and his ambitious plans for Mars colonization, this book dives into Musk's triumphs and failures. It gives a comprehensive overview of his complicated personality and career by discussing not just his accomplishments but also the controversy surrounding him.

We hope that by reading this biography about Elon Musk, you will be inspired to achieve great things or even just simply learn something about the man revolutionizing key industries in today's world. There are questions at the end of each chapter to help you integrate the knowledge gained to your own life. Get ready for an adventure!

Early Years: Elon Musk's Formative Years

Elon was born on June 28, 1971, in Pretoria, South Africa, to a middle-class family as the eldest of three children. His mother, Maye Musk, a Canadian-South African model and nutritionist, was known for her independence, strong work ethic, and commitment to her job, which had a significant impact on Elon's upbringing. For example, she introduced him to computers at an early age. His father, Errol Musk, an engineer, problem solver, and entrepreneur, developed and managed several successful companies and instilled in Elon an entrepreneurial spirit from a young age. For example, he would debate business strategies with Elon as a child to encourage entrepreneurship. They lived in a comfortable environment with a satisfactory balance of personal challenges and academic growth.

Early on, Elon showed exceptional intelligence and curiosity from his passion for programming and science. Elon was deeply affected by the terrible apartheid government of South Africa, which shaped his strong beliefs in justice and equality and made him look for opportunities outside. "I didn't see a future for myself there," Musk later reflected in an interview with *Biography Magazine* (2017). "I wanted to go somewhere that allowed me to pursue my dreams and contribute to something bigger."

A Curious Mind: The Early Traits of Elon Musk

From the beginning, Elon Musk had an insatiable curiosity and a desire to understand the world. His family and friends commented on his focus and determination even when his interests differed from everyone else's. He spent hours and hours reading books, mostly science fiction, history, and philosophy. J.R.R. Tolkien's The Lord of the Rings was the first book that ignited his love for epic quests, and biographies of inventors like Thomas Edison and Benjamin Franklin inspired his entrepreneurial spirit. Isaac Asimov's Foundation series resonated with him the most; he believed science and reason could solve humanity's biggest problems. "I was inspired by the idea that civilization could be preserved and expanded through knowledge and innovation," he told The Verge in 2017.

At 10 years old, Musk's interest in technology took off when his father bought him a Commodore VIC-20, one of the first personal computers. Instead of treating it as a toy, he saw it as an opportunity to learn programming. "There was no one to teach me," he told Rolling Stone in 2017, "so I just figured it out myself." He read the manual and started experimenting, developing his problem-solving skills.

By 12, he had created Blastar, a space-themed video game inspired by the sci-fi books he loved. He sold it to a magazine for $500. This small victory showed his ability to combine creativity with technical skills. It also gave him the confidence to go bigger (Ashlee Vance, 2015).

A Target at School

School was another tough place for Elon. As a bright and introverted kid who loved science fiction and technology, he stood out in ways that made him a target for bullying. His love of books like *The Hitchhiker's Guide to the Galaxy* and his interest in computers were seen as weird by his peers, making him even more isolated.

Musk's intelligence and interests made him stand out, and he struggled to find peers who shared his passions. His love for science fiction and his reading habits made him different from his classmates, and he felt isolated. Peers frequently bullied him and even physically attacked him, once throwing him down a flight of stairs and sending him to the hospital (Ashlee Vance, 2015). But Musk's resilience prevailed. He channeled his energy into learning and creating and was determined to rise above his environment.

After that, he channeled his energy into his passions: self-improvement and technology. The challenges he faced at school taught him grit and self-reliance, which would be essential in his entrepreneurial journey.

What Others Had to Say

Family and a few close friends described Musk as introspective and imaginative. His mother, Maye Musk, once said, "Elon was always lost in thought, constantly coming up with ideas that no one else could see" (Biography Magazine, 2017). While teachers recognized his potential, they frequently perceived him as a dreamer, preferring to envision the future over the present.

One story from Musk's childhood sums up his imagination and boldness. At school, a teacher asked the class what they wanted to be when they grew up. Most kids said doctor or pilot. Musk said, "I want to invent things that change the world." The other kids laughed, but Musk didn't flinch. At the time, people dismissed that statement, but it turned out to be prophetic (Esquire, 2008).

Musk didn't have many friends as a kid, but his intellectual pursuits and determination set him up to be the visionary he would become. The solitude of his childhood only made him more determined to push boundaries and create a future no one else could imagine.

Home Life

Elon's early years were crazy and tough. His dad, Errol, played a crucial role in that. Errol's engineering skills and intelligence taught him practical problem-solving, but the relationship was emotionally charged. Elon has said his dad was "brilliant but emotionally abusive," and that had deeply affected him (*Rolling Stone*, 2017). In a 2017 interview with The New York Times, he said "I had to unlearn certain patterns I learned in childhood. It was a tough environment."

His home life left him with emotional scars but also taught him resilience. Watching his dad's technical skills gave him a foundation in analytical thinking, which he would later use to tackle engineering and business problems. But the psychological toll of growing up in that environment was big. This duality made him determined not only to succeed but also to create environments—personal and professional—that were collaborative and respectful (Ashlee Vance, *Elon Musk: Tesla, SpaceX, and the Quest for a Fantastic Future*, 2015).

Into the Unknown: Elon Musk's Big Leap

At 17, Elon made the life-changing decision to leave South Africa and start fresh in Canada. It was a combination of political conviction and personal desire that drove him to make the move. Growing up in South Africa under apartheid, Elon was deeply opposed to the system of racism and injustice. And mandatory military service for young men under apartheid was something he couldn't live with.

"I didn't want to be part of a system I fundamentally disagreed with," he told Biography Magazine in 2017. "Moving to Canada was a risk, but it gave me the chance to follow my dreams in a place that matched my values."

Starting Fresh in Canada

Musk arrived in Canada with $2,000, a sum likely provided by his parents, and a determination to make it work. He used his mom Maye's Canadian citizenship to get in and start building a new life. His early days were tough and resourceful, and he took on physical jobs like cleaning boilers and cutting logs to survive. He later said this period of hardship taught him the value of resilience and hard work (Ashlee Vance, *Elon Musk: Tesla, SpaceX, and the Quest for a Fantastic Future*, 2015).

Canada gave Musk a clean slate and a way to pursue his academic and entrepreneurial dreams. It was here that he started building the foundation for his future success, driven by an unshakeable belief that he could do something amazing.

Musk enrolled at Queen's University in Kingston, Ontario, and quickly stood out. Known for his work ethic and curiosity, he approached his studies with a desire to learn and make connections. It was at Queen's that he met his future wife, Justine Wilson, and other people who would play big roles in his life.

At Queen's, Musk developed a reputation for being creative and not being afraid to question the status quo, a habit that would serve him well later in his career.

University of Pennsylvania

After two years at Queen's, Musk transferred to the University of Pennsylvania (UPenn) to further his education. At UPenn, he studied a dual degree in physics and economics, a combination that reflected his desire to marry technical innovation with business savvy. He graduated from the College of Arts and Sciences with a degree in physics and from the Wharton School, one of the world's top business schools.

The training in these fields gave Musk a unique skill set. Physics taught him problem-solving and a scientific approach to challenges, while economics gave him the tools to navigate business and finance. This dual expertise would later serve him well in ventures like Tesla, SpaceX and SolarCity, where technical innovation had to align with market reality.

While at UPenn, Musk showed his entrepreneurial tendencies in unusual ways. He and a roommate rented a 10-bedroom house and turned it into a nightclub on weekends. For $5 entry, they made enough to cover the rent and gave students a social outlet.

This showed Musk's ability to spot opportunities and maximize resources even in college. And his willingness to take calculated risks, a habit that would serve him well in business and innovation.

A Path Forward

Musk graduated from UPenn in 1997 with a clear direction. The combination of physics and economics gave him a view of the world and a roadmap for his career. Looking back on his education, Musk has often said the key is to pursue knowledge that applies to real-world problems.

"Education is about solving problems," Musk told Esquire in 2015, "Whether it's understanding the universe or creating a sustainable future, it's to make life better for humanity."

All of this laid the groundwork for what was to come. He was brave, flexible, and unrelenting in his pursuit of a better world. Musk credits his early struggles with making him resilient and driven. "I didn't have a trust fund. I had to create something from nothing," he told Wired in 2015. Those early years helped Musk develop the problem-solving mindset and willingness to take risks that would later be the hallmark of his entrepreneurial ventures.

His early interest in space, born from science fiction and childhood tinkering, has been the foundation of his lifelong goal to make humanity a multi-planetary species.

End of Chapter 1 - Deep Insights into Elon Musk's Formative Years

Chapter 1 - Quotes from Musk

- ❖ **"I was raised by books. Books, and then my parents."** — *Rolling Stone*, 2017.
  In this interview he talks about how literature played a bigger role in his intellectual development than traditional parenting.

- ❖ **"I just had this existential crisis. I was trying to figure out what does it all mean? What's the purpose of life?"** — *Rolling Stone*, 2017.
  This quote shows his early interest in the big questions of life which would later inform his goals to solve global and interplanetary problems.

- ❖ **"If something is important enough, even if the odds are against you, you should still do it."** — *TED*, 2013.
  He said this in a TED Talk, where he explains the philosophy that drives him to take on impossible ventures, from SpaceX to Tesla.

Chapter 1 - Interesting Facts

- ❖ **Errol Musk and the Emerald Mine:** Musk's dad owned an emerald mine in Zambia. A fact that has raised questions about Musk's upbringing and his later claim to have started from nothing (Business Insider, 2018).

- ❖ **Voracious Reader:** As a kid, Musk read 2 books a day. Science fiction, encyclopedias, you name it (Biography Magazine, 2018).

- ❖ **Hearing Concerns:** As a kid, Musk was so lost in thought that his parents took him to get his hearing tested, thinking he was deaf (Ashlee Vance, *Elon Musk: Tesla, SpaceX, and the Quest for a Fantastic Future*).

- **Immigration and Odd Jobs:** At 17, Musk moved to Canada with $2,000 and did odd jobs – cleaning boilers and cutting logs – to support himself. He learned the value of hard work that would serve him well later (Biography Magazine, 2018).

Chapter 1 - Key Points

- **The Curiosity:** His reading habits shaped his critical thinking and ability to see the future. Books like The Hitchhiker's Guide to the Galaxy made him think of problem solving and optimism for humanity (Time Magazine, 2018)

- **Overcoming Obstacles:** Growing up in apartheid South Africa, he was bullied and socially isolated. One particularly violent incident left him in hospital, but these experiences built the resilience he would later use as an entrepreneur (Ashlee Vance).

- **Early Entrepreneur:** Selling Blastar at 12 years old showed his ability to spot opportunities in technology, which he would later turn into a career (Rolling Stone, 2017).

- **Big Questions:** Since early on, he was obsessed with the big questions. These questions would later inform his ventures to solve humanity's biggest problems, like sustainable energy and space travel (The Verge, 2017).

Chapter 1 - Questions to Ponder

1. Musk credited books with broadening his worldview. What resources or habits have helped you learn about new possibilities in your life?

2. Musk's challenges, such as bullying and isolation, shaped his resilience. How have your own struggles influenced your ability to persevere?

3. Musk's ambitious goals stemmed from his existential reflections. What big questions drive your ambitions or life goals?

4. Musk took significant risks as a young immigrant. Have you ever taken a leap of faith? What did you learn from the experience?

Chapter 1 - Activities

1. **Vision Exercise**
   Write down your long-term goals, including the steps to get there. What drives these goals? Like Musk, create meaningful impact.

2. **Problem Solving Challenge**
   Choose a daily problem and create a plan to solve it. How does Musk solve global problems?

3. **Resilience Journal**
   Write about a time you faced a challenge and how you overcame it. What traits or habits helped you? Like Musk.

4. **Read Outside Your Comfort Zone**
   Pick a book not in your usual genre (sci-fi or philosophy) to stretch your mind like Musk does.

The Early Career of Elon Musk: A Journey of Vision, Struggle, and Resilience

Elon Musk's story is one of ambition, relentless determination, and boundless curiosity. Before becoming a global icon for innovation, Musk's early career was marked by bold decisions, significant challenges, and inspiring triumphs that laid the foundation for his transformative ventures in space exploration, renewable energy, and artificial intelligence. Musk graduated in 1997 with a clear vision for the future. Reflecting on this period, Musk once said, *"Education isn't just about absorbing information; it's about solving problems and creating the future you want to live in"* (*Esquire*, 2015).

Zip2: The Digital Pioneer

In 1995, Elon founded Zip2 with his brother Kimbal and business partner Greg Kouri in Silicon Valley. The idea was revolutionary for its time: an online city guide that combined maps with business listings so local businesses could have a presence on the rapidly growing internet. Online directories are now commonplace, but in the mid-1990s it was new, so Zip2 was the first in the digitalisation of local advertising.

Elon's commitment to Zip2 was total. He lived frugally, worked 24/7, slept on a beanbag in the office, and showered at the local YMCA to save on living costs. He told Esquire in 2008: "I didn't have a house for the first year. I put everything I had into making Zip2 work."

This all-in approach would be a pattern for the rest of his career; he was willing to make personal sacrifices for his ventures. Zip2 was not just a business; he wanted to solve a real problem by connecting users to local resources through technology.

Investors were initially sceptical of the Zip2 business model. The internet was still in its infancy, and many saw it as a niche tool, not a transformational medium. But Elon's persistence and technical skills convinced investors to give Zip2 a go. He was able to explain the internet and how it could be applied to local businesses to key partners.

Zip2 eventually got traction and landed big clients like The New York Times and The Chicago Tribune. These partnerships proved the business model and brought much-needed credibility and revenue. The company's success was a testament to Elon's ability to see trends and capitalise on emerging opportunities in the tech world.

Elon's leadership style was key to getting Zip2 moving but often caused friction with others. His intensity and hands-on approach clashed with the board of directors, and he was replaced as CEO in 1996. While this was a personal setback, he later reflected on it as a valuable learning experience: "It taught me that great ideas need great leadership to sustain them. You can't do everything alone" (Wired, 2004).

This experience would shape his approach to leadership in his future ventures; he would learn to balance ambition with collaboration.

In 1999 Compaq bought Zip2 for $307 million, a big milestone in Elon's career. He got $22 million out of it which would be the foundation for his next ventures. He didn't see this as the end but as a springboard to go even bigger.

Elon looks back on Zip2 as a critical part of his journey. It not only taught him the difficulties of entrepreneurship but also that technology could change the way people interact with the world.

X.com and the Birth of PayPal

Musk used the Zip2 money to go after the financial industry and created X.com and then PayPal. This would be the start of his multi-industry disruption.

In 1999 Musk used $10 million of his earnings to launch the original X.com, an online financial services company to disrupt banking. Musk wanted a frictionless, user-friendly system to do secure transactions.

The company faced intense competition and internal disagreements over strategy. In 2000 X.com merged with Confinity then rebranded the company as PayPal and it quickly became the leading online payment system in the world.

In 2002, eBay bought PayPal for $1.5 billion in stock, a big moment for the payments industry and for Elon's career. At the time, PayPal was the biggest online payment platform, and money was moving in a whole new way. Elon was one of the largest shareholders and walked away with $180 million—a nice little nest egg to fund his future projects (Rolling Stone, 2017).

This was big not just because of the cash but also because of the lessons he learned during his time at PayPal. He knew about scalability, user experience and the power of disruption in traditional industries (Ashlee Vance, *Elon Musk: Tesla, SpaceX, and the Quest for a Fantastic Future*, 2015).

Turning Setbacks into Opportunities

The sale of PayPal wasn't just about the money for Musk – it was a pivot point that allowed him to reorient his goals. While Musk had many problems at PayPal – being replaced as CEO was one of them – he came out of it more determined and ready for the big leagues (Biography Magazine, 2017).

In interviews, he calls this period a time of rebalancing. He could have coasted on the wealth the acquisition provided, but instead, he chose to double down on risk and ambition. He used his PayPal money to fund three new ventures:

1. SpaceX (2002) – A private space company to reduce space exploration costs and make life multi-planetary.
2. Tesla Motors (2004) – An electric car company that would become the global leader in sustainable energy.
3. SolarCity (2006) – A solar energy services company to promote renewable energy adoption (Esquire, 2008).

In his own words: "I could have bought a private island and relaxed for the rest of my life, but I wanted to tackle the biggest challenges facing humanity" (Rolling Stone, 2017).

PayPal's Legacy

PayPal's sale to eBay and its global adoption as the standard for online payments showed the power of disruption. For Musk, it was a crash course in scaling technology, managing growth, and dealing with organizational challenges. It also taught him that technology could be a force for tremendous change (Rolling Stone, 2017).

In retrospect PayPal was more than a financial success for Musk—it was the school in which he learned the skills and mentality to go big. As he said: "PayPal was a good experience, but I wanted to build companies that could change the world big time" (Wired, 2006).

The Influencers in Musk's Journey

Elon Musk's rise to fame as an entrepreneur wasn't a solo act. Along the way, he was surrounded by a network of family, friends, mentors and allies. These relationships helped shape his early ventures and provided emotional and practical support during the toughest times of his career.

Family: A Bond of Support and Shared Vision

At the core of Musk's journey was his brother Kimbal. The two had a special bond built on their shared entrepreneurial spirit and desire to change the world. Kimbal co-founded Zip2 with Elon in 1995 and was part of the business strategy and vision. Their complementary skills—Elon's tech genius and Kimbal's business brain—were the secret to Zip2's success.

Kimbal was also a source of emotional support. In a 2015 interview, Elon said: "Kimbal believed in what we were doing when others didn't. That belief got us through the tough times." (Ashlee Vance, 2015)

Even after Zip2, Kimbal was a considerable influence in Elon's life and supported him through Tesla and SpaceX. Their partnership shows the power of family in overcoming obstacles and achieving a shared vision.

Mentors and Allies: Influencing Musk's Entrepreneurial Path

Elon Musk's journey was also shaped by a few key mentors and allies who provided guidance, resources, and inspiration at key moments in his career.

- **Greg Kouri:** Co-founder of Zip2 and close friend, Greg Kouri was part of the early days of the company. Beyond the financial investment, Kouri was a source of emotional support during the long years of building a startup. He believed in Elon's vision and was a steady presence when doubts or obstacles arose. According to Biography Magazine (2017), Kouri's belief in Elon's potential was a reminder of the importance of trust in business partnerships.

- **Peter Thiel:** Fellow entrepreneur and co-founder of Confinity, Peter Thiel, was instrumental in Musk's development during the creation of PayPal. The merger between X.com (Musk's company) and Confinity brought Musk and Thiel together and formed a partnership that changed online payments. Thiel's experience and strategic thinking helped Musk navigate the Silicon Valley startup scene.
  - Musk said in a 2006 Wired interview, "Peter was both a partner and a mentor. He could see ten steps ahead. He taught me how to think strategically, which was critical for PayPal's growth and success."

- **Larry Page:** Though their partnership came later in Musk's career, Google co-founder Larry Page is another substantial influence in Musk's network. Page and Musk love technology's ability to solve the world's biggest problems and often chat and inspire each other's big projects.

Musk learned some of the most important lessons of his career from these relationships:

1. **Collaboration:** Musk's relationships with Kimbal, Kouri and Thiel showed him the value of teamwork.
2. **Strategic thinking and vision:** Mentors like Peter Thiel taught Musk to think long-term and take risks.
3. **Trust and support:** Whether from family or allies, Musk's journey shows the power of trust and backing in overcoming obstacles.

As he said: "Success is rarely a solo effort. The people around you can lift you or pull you down. I've been lucky to have great people in my corner" (Rolling Stone, 2017).

These relationships gave Musk the resources to succeed and made him the person he is today – a bold innovator who keeps pushing the boundaries.

End of Chapter 2 - Deep Insights: The Early Career of Elon Musk

Chapter 2 - Quotes from Musk

Elon's early life and career is a treasure trove of information about his thinking, values and problem solving. Here are some quotes from him that give us a glimpse into his journey. These quotes are not just about him, but for you to overcome your challenges and be creative.

- ❖ **Leaving South Africa and Going Where the Cool Stuff Is**
    - ○ "I wanted to be where the cool stuff was happening." (Esquire, 2015) He left his home country at 17, so he could be surrounded by innovation and creativity.
    - ○ "I learned to make something remarkable with limited resources." (Biography, 2015) Working odd jobs to support himself taught Musk resilience and resourcefulness, values he would carry into his entrepreneurial ventures.

- ❖ **Risk and Optimism**
    - ○ "I believe in being optimistic and making big bets. If you're not failing, you're not innovating." (Esquire, 2008) This sums up Musk's fearless approach to big challenges even when failure seems certain.

- ❖ **Persistence**
    - ○ "Every failure is an opportunity to learn." (Wired, 2015) Musk views setbacks as stepping stones, he has a growth mindset and is committed to continuous improvement.

- ❖ **Long Term**
    - ○ "Think big, think ahead, act." (Biography, 2015) This is the theme of his whole life, from his early entrepreneurial ventures to Tesla and SpaceX.

Chapter 2 - Interesting Facts

- ❖ **Coding at Night:** Musk wrote most of Zip2's code himself, 20-hour days.
- ❖ **Early Clean Energy Interest:** At Penn he researched electric vehicles and renewable energy as part of his academic projects.
- ❖ **Sleeping on the Floor:** He slept on the floor of his office to save money in the early days of Zip2.
- ❖ **X.com's Original Idea:** X.com was originally supposed to be a full bank, offering loans and credit in addition to payment processing.

Chapter 2 - Key Points

- ❖ **Resilience:** Musk's Zip2 experience showed resilience. Musk persevered despite early internet investors doubting his ideas and the board removing him as CEO. His focus on Zip2 and hard work to expand the company kept him from giving up. His entrepreneurial style was characterized by overcoming obstacles.
- ❖ **Vision:** Musk's Zip2 work showed his vision. Musk observed how digital could affect local companies and advertising through online directories when the internet was new. Zip2 won big clients like The New York Times and The Chicago Tribune to validate his vision.
- ❖ **Adaptability:** He learned from his failures. After losing his CEO position at Zip 2, he realized the importance of ambition over teamwork. He would use his failures to evolve and apply those lessons in his future endeavours.

Chapter 2 - Questions to Ponder

1. How did early life challenges prepare him for later life obstacles?
2. What was the role of teamwork in his early wins?

3. How can failure lead to long term success?

Chapter 2 - Activities

1. **Create a Startup Plan:** Draft a business plan for an innovative idea inspired by Musk's ventures.

2. **Research Emerging Trends:** Identify a technology or industry that you believe will shape the future and explore how it might evolve.

3. **Overcoming Challenges Exercise:** Write about a personal challenge and how you overcame it, drawing inspiration from Musk's resilience.

Later Career: Transforming the World, One Idea at a Time

SpaceX: The Path to Interplanetary Life

Vision and Beginnings

Elon Musk's vision of "getting mankind to Mars" started as a utopian dream in 2001. At the time, Musk was already a successful entrepreneur, having co-founded PayPal, but his ambitions extended far beyond digital payments. He envisioned a future where humanity could thrive as a multi-planetary species. His ambitious notion extended beyond space, aiming to link exploration with everyday life codes.

To deliver Mars, a tiny greenhouse designed to grow rice or wheat, as a vote of confidence on public display, to restore global interest in space exploration. Musk hoped the project would inspire humanity to reach for the stars again. However, widespread skepticism met his enthusiasm. As he later recalled during a 2012 interview on 60 Minutes, "They talked to me like I didn't know what I was talking about." Critics dismissed him as naive and ill-equipped for such a monumental task.

"Why not build the rockets myself?" Musk, determined to dispel his doubters, took control of the situation. He raised $100 million from his treasury and, in 2002, founded SpaceX (Space Exploration Technologies Corp.).

From a small office in El Segundo, California, Musk gathered a team of top engineers who shared a vision of making space economically and environmentally friendly. SpaceX adopted a "first principles" approach to rocket design, breaking it down to its basic components to reduce cost and steps while increasing efficiency. The company's success was attributed to a culture of innovation, long hours (overtime), and resourcefulness—doing more with less.

Elon's famous saying, "If something is important enough, you do it, come hell or high water" (first said in his 2013 TED Talk) is the battle cry for the SpaceX team. Through sheer will and determination, they turned an audacious idea into a concrete goal: going to Mars.

From Near Failure to Groundbreaking Success

SpaceX's path to success was not smooth. The company faced numerous near-catastrophic failures that nearly led to its demise before it had a chance to launch. Between 2006 and 2008, the company had three consecutive rocket launch failures with the first vehicle, the Falcon 1. Each of those failures damaged the company's reputation and drained its bank account, putting the company on the brink of bankruptcy. Musk had put his entire life savings into SpaceX, and every failure was putting it out of business.

The pressure was intense. By the fourth launch attempt, SpaceX was out of money. Musk later admitted in interviews that the company's existence was on the line. If the fourth Falcon 1 launch failed, it would be the end of SpaceX. The team invested heavily, and, on 28 September 2008, Falcon 1 achieved orbit and initiated the initial phase of space exploration. SpaceX was the first privately funded company to do so, a milestone that changed everything.

In a 2017 Rolling Stone interview, Musk said, "It was one of the best days of my life." He added, "I cried tears of joy. It was validation for all we had sacrificed." The successful crewed flight saved SpaceX and proved that private companies could design and operate commercially in an industry that was previously a government monopoly. The timing couldn't have been better. Almost immediately after the Falcon 1 launch, NASA awarded SpaceX a $1.6 billion contract to resupply the International Space Station (ISS). Under this contract, SpaceX got financial stability and a track record and could grow rapidly. It began a new era of space exploration where private companies could be at the center.

Game-Changing Innovations

SpaceX (best known for its work on reusability) has made its greatest contribution to space exploration. Rockets were disposable machines for many years, and each launch cost hundreds of thousands, if not millions, of dollars in hardware lost or wasted during re-entry. Musk saw this as a major inefficiency. He compared it with throwing away a brand-new aircraft after every flight. Not wanting to break this paradigm, Musk and his crew built the Falcon 9, a rocket that can land and fly back into space multiple times.

The road to reusability was not without its challenges. Initial attempts to land the Falcon 9 booster were spectacularly unsuccessful, resulting in fiery blowups of the booster and flyaway landings. Nevertheless, in December 2015, SpaceX made its first landing with a Falcon 9. This success revolutionized the economics of space flight in an unprecedented way, thus making space cheaper and, consequently, more available. Reusability decreases costs by 10 times, Musk went on to state during a 2015 Bloomberg interview, "It's the key to making space accessible to everyone."

Since then, SpaceX has refined the science of reusability in ways that have served Falcon 9's liquid stage, which has been recovered and reused hundreds of times. This technology has not only saved hundreds of millions of dollars (US), but also opened up the possibility for SpaceX to pursue significant goals, like launching communications and Earth observation satellites and partnering with NASA to build crewed missions.

Mars and Beyond: Starship

SpaceX's biggest project to date is Starship, a fully reusable spacecraft that will take humans to Mars and beyond. At 120 meters tall, Starship is the biggest and most powerful rocket ever built. It's the key to Musk's goal of having a self-sustaining human city on Mars by the 2030s.

A starship is unlike any spacecraft ever built. Its versatile design allows it to carry up to 100 people and cargo. Reusability is key to making interplanetary travel economically viable. SpaceX has already flown several Starship prototypes, each bringing us closer to Mars colonization.

For Musk, it's personal. In a 2020 TED Talk, he said, "We can't stay on Earth forever. Something will make life here impossible. Mars is the hope for a second chapter of human history." Starship isn't just about Mars; it's about humanity's long-term survival by having a backup plan for life off Earth.

Cultural and Scientific Impact

The world has been mesmerized by SpaceX's space achievements which have changed the way we think about space. SpaceX has started a new era of innovation and competition in space and has shown that private companies can achieve what was previously only possible for governments. A new generation of innovators are being inspired to push boundaries by SpaceX's feats.

By pursuing the Mars colonization vision, Elon's unrelenting drive has made space more accessible and humanity's goal of becoming a multiplanetary species more achievable. SpaceX is still a big player in space exploration because it lands rockets that can be used again, sends missions to Mars, and brings people to the International Space Station.

SpaceX was able to land the Falcon 9 on a drone ship after several failed tries. This shows that hard work and creativity can make the impossible possible.

Tesla: From Startup to Sustainability Giant

In 2004, Tesla Motors was a tiny startup founded by Martin Eberhard and Marc Tarpenning. Their goal was to build sexy, high-performance electric vehicles (EVs) that would compete with gas cars. At the time, EVs were seen as impractical—boxy, slow, and for the eco-conscious fringe.

Elon joined Tesla as an early investor, putting in $6.5M in Series A and becoming chairperson of the board. Although he didn't create the company, Elon's strategic vision quickly overtook Tesla. He was determined to prove EVs could be faster, more efficient, and more desirable than common cars.

There were three steps to Elon's plan for Tesla's growth and each would move the company closer to its goal of accelerating the world's transition to sustainable energy:

Step 1: Develop a high-end, low-volume sports car to generate buzz: The first step was to build a high-quality electric vehicle (EV) that would get people's attention and prove EVs could be innovative and desirable. This led to the Tesla Roadster, a sexy high-performance sports car that would show off the electric powertrain. By targeting the luxury niche, Tesla could establish the brand with early adopters and generate the funds for the next stage.

Step 2: Use profits to fund a more affordable luxury sedan: With the Roadster's success, Tesla moved into the second stage of its plan. This was to use the profits and technology from the Roadster to build a more affordable luxury car. The result was the Tesla Model S, a game-changing sedan with range, performance, and technology. The Model S was key to Tesla's journey as it started to bring in a wider customer base while continuing to push the limits of what EVs could do.

Step 3: Transition to mass-market, affordable EVs to achieve true sustainability: The final stage of the plan was the most audacious—affordable electric vehicles for the masses. Tesla released the Model 3, a more mainstream EV for the broad market. This was the key to sustainability: making EVs available to more people and reducing fossil fuel dependence. The Model 3 was Tesla's transition from a luxury brand to a global automaker.

This was the secret master plan, as Musk called it in his 2006 blog post "The Secret Tesla Motors Master Plan (just between you and me)". It shows Musk's long-term thinking and commitment to a sustainable future. Each stage of the plan was a stepping stone for Tesla's growth and a statement about the company's values of innovation, scalability, and environmental responsibility.

The Tesla Roadster: Revolutionizing the EV Market

The Tesla Roadster was more than a car; it was a game changer for the electric vehicle (EV) industry. The Roadster, introduced in 2008, marked Tesla's entry into the automobile sector and dramatically stated what EVs may do. The Roadster, built on the chassis of a Lotus Elise, perfectly combines high-performance engineering with compelling looks. While it looked good, the Roadster was fast. Incredibly fast. 0-60 in 3.7 seconds, faster than many of the sports cars on the market. It killed the myth that electric cars were slow and boring and could compete with gas cars.

The Roadster stood out because of its range. With its advanced lithium-ion battery cells, the Roadster had a record-breaking 200+ miles of range. For the time, which was a big deal. The Roadster proved that electric cars could be good at all three - usefulness, performance, and looks - when many EVs were slow and ranged. For Tesla and the entire EV industry, it changed everything. It raised the bar for what electric cars could do.

But the Roadster's journey was far from smooth. Just getting started, Tesla was still struggling with manufacturing. Early Roadster models had quality control issues, so it was hard to make an electric car that was pretty, fast, and innovative. For example, some consumers reported issues with fit and finish, while others encountered mechanical failures that necessitated costly repairs. These setbacks stretched Tesla's resources, and the business soon found itself going through cash at an alarming rate.

In 2008, Elon Musk took over as CEO of Tesla as the company faced rising hurdles. Because Musk had previously invested heavily in the company, he was active in production. He worked tirelessly and slept on the manufacturing floor to ensure that the Roadster matched Tesla's ambitious standards of quality and innovation. It paid off; the crew overcame some early production challenges, and the Roadster was everything it was supposed to be.

The Roadster had an impact beyond its speed and style. It became a cultural icon that showed how people around the world were changing their minds about electric cars. Musk talked about the Roadster's importance in an interview with The Guardian in 2018. He said, "The Roadster wasn't merely a car; it was a bold statement that electric cars could surpass petrol cars in performance and aesthetics." The Roadster challenged the idea that electric cars were not as good as regular cars, starting a new age of environmentally friendly transportation.

The Roadster's success enabled Tesla to expand and develop in the future. It helped the corporation establish itself as a clean energy leader and provided expertise in manufacturing electric vehicles. The next models, particularly the Model S, were influenced by what they learned from the Roadster. So, the company became even stronger in the EV market.

It's clear the Tesla Roadster was more than a car; it was a disruptor. It proved electric cars could be fast, beautiful, and practical, forcing innovation in the auto industry. Despite hurdles, the Roadster's legacy lives on as a symbol of what is possible when technology and imagination come together to challenge conventional standards. The Roadster revolutionized the EV market and demonstrated that sustainable mobility could be both ecologically benign and exciting.

Tesla Model S and Scaling the Vision

The launch of the Tesla Model S in 2012 marked a pivotal moment not only for the company but for the entire automotive industry. That was not only an electric car but was a luxury sedan that overcame many misconceptions of what an EV could do. The Model S succeeded in changing the perception that EVs were little more than small, limited-range niche products for extremely environmentally conscious, rich consumers.

The Model S stood out with a suite of groundbreaking features that set it apart from anything else on the market.

- ❖ **Unmatched Range:** With a long-range battery, it allowed the vehicle to travel up to 400 miles on a single charge—a world record for an electric vehicle at that time. This relieved one of the main problems that consumers had regarding electric vehicles (EVs)—range anxiety.

- ❖ **Advanced Autopilot Technology:** By utilizing the Model S, Tesla became market- and industry-leading in the direction of Tesla's active driver assistance (Tesla's "autopilot" technology), for which Tesla earned a several-year advantage over competing commercially available semi-autonomous driving prototypes.

- ❖ **Innovative Design:** Its clean, low-key interior was dominated solely by a 17-in screen, which in effect governed most elements of the car's operation, instead of a traditional grouping of buttons and knobs, with an elegant, user-friendly, and intuitive interface. This design philosophy became a hallmark of Tesla vehicles.

The Model S soon received a massive amount of positive publicity, as it showed that sustainability could co-exist with performance and aesthetics. It earned the title Car of the Year 2013 in MotorTrend, and it also achieved critical and consumer praise. As one of the earliest achievements, the Model S has provided the first electric vehicle class to reach a level of sales volume above its same-class in-line gasoline-powered luxury sedan counterparts and thus has illustrated a tectonic shift in consumer preference and served as a forerunner of a more general adoption trend toward vehicle-based electrical machine-powered systems.

It was a Tesla time, a Tesla achievement, and, as a result, has been the big opening of the floodgates for Tesla's innovative growth strategies. However, achieving this growth came with significant challenges. Scaling production necessitated changing from a niche car company to a mass production juggernaut, a change that Tesla's CEO at the time, Elon Musk, went on to characterize as "production hell. I was sleeping on the factory floor, working 120-hour weeks. It was excruciating, but failure wasn't an option."

Despite the immense challenges, Tesla persevered. Having weathered this storm, the company is in a position that is not only strong but is now better prepared to compete with the rest of the EV marketplace in the future with the Model 3 (value price), Model X SUV, and Model Y crossover. The experience gained in the production ramp-up of the Model S would turn out to be a very interesting installment in Tesla's road to becoming one of the world's leading automotive companies.

Model S was more than just a car; it was the beating heart of a revolution. It changed the reality for what consumers can experience in driving an electric vehicle, and it showed it is not necessary for electric vehicles to forego status relative to driving an internal combustion engine (ICE) vehicle in order to compete. Even more significantly, it established Tesla's leadership in moving towards an environmentally sustainable future, and in doing so, has set an example for the entirety of an industry to follow.

Building Gigafactories: Tesla's Global Expansion

Elon Musk's vision for Tesla has never been just about cars – it's about accelerating the world to sustainable energy. At the heart of that is battery production, the key to making electric vehicles (EVs) accessible and affordable for the masses. So, Musk created Gigafactories, huge facilities for mass-producing batteries and other essential components (Tesla, 2023).

It began with the first Gigafactory in Nevada, which launched in 2016. This structure was the largest in the world in terms of footprint, demonstrating Musk's ambition (Forbes, 2021). Here, Tesla produced battery cells for its EVs and products like the Powerwall and Powerpack, which help homes and businesses store renewable energy better. However, Musk's plans never focused on just one location. Knowing global demand for EVs and sustainable energy solutions would explode, Tesla rapidly built its Gigafactories worldwide.

The Shanghai Gigafactory, which launched in 2019, was Tesla's bet on one of the largest and fastest growing EV markets (Bloomberg, 2019). Then Berlin, to solidify Tesla's presence in Europe with a state-of-the-art facility focused on efficiency and innovation (CNBC, 2021). And most recently the Texas Gigafactory to cement Musk's vision of a sustainable energy future for North America, with innovative production and lower costs (Tesla, 2022).

Beyond production, the Gigafactories have had an enormous impact on local economies. They created thousands of high-quality jobs, attracting top talent from engineering, manufacturing and tech (Reuters, 2020). They served as a catalyst for green energy developments, inspiring others to follow suit (The Guardian, 2021).

Elon Musk refers to Tesla's Gigafactories as "the machine that builds the machine," which summarizes his strategy for expanding innovation to solve global issues (Musk, 2016). Musk has transformed the Gigafactories into more than just production facilities, incorporating advanced automation, artificial intelligence, and renewable energy systems.

Tesla's Impact on Sustainability

Tesla's mission—"to accelerate energy transition to sustainable energy"—has brought about change on a magnitude that not only revolutionized the car business but also the global energy production and storage infrastructure. The impact of the company goes far beyond the vehicles; it affects companies and people to redefine renewable energy and sustainability solutions. Tesla has been leading the way in major technological advances and has thus already grasped the position at the top of the ecological and social improvement wave towards a cleaner, greener world and society. Here are some of the company's most noteworthy contributions:

- **Mass Adoption of EVs:** Tesla has disrupted the electric vehicle (EV) market, driving mainstream adoption of EVs by overcoming barriers to their widespread use in the past, including range anxiety and lack of charging capability. By commercializing designs, Model S, Model 3, Model X, and Model Y, Tesla has established that electric vehicles (EVs) can be high performance, stylish, and affordable in a broad market. The market position of Tesla has forced traditional automakers (Ford, GM, and Volkswagen) to go electric to the tune of billions of dollars and with a strategy for putting all-electric vehicles in the hands of customers. This competitive development has driven the industry-wide shift to electric vehicles and therefore the global drive towards a clean-air world.

- **Battery Innovation:** Through significant reduction of battery fabrication cost and energy consumption, Tesla has reduced the cost of electric vehicles and made them feasible to travel longer distances. These developments are not limited to the vehicle but also to energy storage applications embodied in Tesla battery technology. Devices, such as Powerwall and Powerpack, facilitated the use and storage of renewable energy in the residential, business, and utility sectors, respectively, thereby facilitating the use and deployment of solar and wind power in the daily energy utilization of a typical household. Tesla's Gigafactories, massive production facilities designed to scale battery manufacturing, are pivotal in meeting the soaring demand for advanced energy storage. These facilities, and others, also produce batteries for grid storage applications and new applications such as aerospace that obviously reveal Tesla's breadth of societal impact in different industries than just the automobile industry.

- ❖ **Solar Energy:** Tesla Energy, the division for renewable energy of Tesla, has already changed the way that individuals and companies create and store solar energy:
    - o Tesla's Powerwall and Powerpack appliances are efficient energy storage devices designed for homes and businesses to lessen reliance on the existing power grids. In regions at risk of losing power often, such as California, the Powerwall is a game changer, providing backup and energy independence to tens of millions of consumers.
    - o Tesla built the largest lithium-ion battery in the world in South Australia is among the most noteworthy accomplishments. Designed to address the region's frequent blackouts, this ground-breaking project was finished in 2017 and has since improved grid reliability and saved millions of dollars in energy expenses. Tesla successfully honored Musk's bold pledge to create the battery within 100 days or it would be free (source: CNBC, "Elon Musk's promise to fix South Australia's power crisis").
    - o The Tesla Solar Roof is a revolutionary product that combines traditional roofing materials with energy-generating solar tiles. Unlike standard rooftop solar panels, the Solar Roof integrates renewable energy into the home's design. The adoption has been slower than expected due to high production costs, installation challenges, and the learning curve of new technology.
    - o In 2021, Tesla launched the Virtual Power Plant (VPP) pilot in California to show off the power of decentralized energy. By linking Powerwall owners into one network, the VPP allows participating homes to feed in electricity

during peak demand, creating a shared energy bank that helps stabilize the grid.

- Elon has been talking about clean, distributed energy for years and envisions a future where every home contributes to the grid, not just consumes from it. During Tesla's 2021 Earnings Call, he said, "This is a glimpse into the future of decentralized energy production. Every home can be a tiny power plant." The VPP pilot is already working in areas like California, where energy demand and blackout risk are high. If successful, it will pave the way for similar systems to be rolled out globally and support the transition to renewable energy.

A Broader Vision for Tesla

As Elon Musk stated, "Tesla isn't simply a vehicle company; it's a renewable energy company. Our goal is to enable society to grow more sustainable" (Musk, 2016). Tesla is working on solutions to some of the most serious issues of our day, including renewable energy, global warming, and transportation options. This is leading to a global shift towards sustainability and renewable energy, which the firm is influencing in many different ways.

Tesla remains a driving force in innovation and sustainable development, solidifying its role as a global leader in transformative change. Electric vehicles, battery storage, or solar energy solutions, the company is taking humanity one step closer to a world powered by clean energy. In an era when businesses and governments are pushing back against climate change, Tesla's efforts represent a powerful example of how technology, innovation, and vision may bring about lasting, beneficial change.

Tesla embodies the concepts of eco-friendly living, technical innovation, and interacting with well-established corporate sectors. Tesla is changing the way we think about sustainability with its many solutions. Tesla made electric vehicles mainstream, pushing the boundaries of what's possible in terms of performance, design and range.

Autonomous Driving: The Future of Transportation

Tesla's flagship innovation is the Full Self-Driving (FSD) system that is in ongoing development. According to the principles of its Autopilot system, FSD is supposed to give vehicles the ability to drive on the road autonomously (without driver intervention). Automotive safety driving systems of various types are featured on Tesla vehicles based on comprehensive on-board hardware. The system uses real-time information from the external environment to "train", continuously improving the driving machine's behavior. Using this hardware/software integration, not only could the convenience still be enhanced, but they are also advocated to be substantial in road safety and efficient, respectively.

Tesla's research in autonomous driving has been an extended and significant step forward. It has decisive implications for self-driving cars and the limits of innovation:

- ❖ **2014:** In keeping pace with evolving times, Tesla, equipped with a feature-rich driver-assistance system (ADAS), brought into existence for the first time an innovative capability of driving functionalities, the driving-assistant system (Autopilot), that integrates adaptive cruise control, auto emergency braking, and lane-tracking features to improve the efficiency of driving. This marked a key milestone in bringing semi-autonomous driving to the mainstream market. Integrating these capabilities, Tesla offered the driving experience an increase in safety and ease of use, which prepared the way for more sophisticated autonomous technologies.

- ❖ **2016:** Tesla's boldness was evident in its use of FSD hardware on all its vehicles—even if its corresponding software was not yet available. Elon Musk has called this "future-proofing" the fleet; in other words, Tesla vehicles would be prepared for the next technological step by releasing future software updates as the technology evolved. This proactive approach made Tesla stand out as a leader in the autonomous vehicle industry and demonstrated its commitment to innovation, even in the face of uncertainty.

- ❖ **2020:** Tesla opened the beta version of its FSD software to a few technically qualified drivers and allowed real-world testing over various conditions. For this reason, this was especially relevant to obtain relevant user feedback that Tesla used as input to train and evolve the road-handling dynamics of the system. As a result of the beta program launch, a discussion has also emerged on ethical and technical issues related to self-driving systems and the fact that pure autonomous vehicles cannot be reached.

Tesla's journey into self-driving cars shows how hard it works to come up with new ideas and how seriously it wants to change the future of transportation.

Elon Musk has long pushed for FSD to change the world. In a 2021 tweet, he said, "Self-driving will fundamentally transform cities, reduce traffic fatalities, and reclaim hours of daily commuting time for millions." Tesla dreams of a future where self-driving cars not only make life easier, but also change the way cities are built, reduce traffic, and save lives through better, smarter driving technology.

As Tesla keeps improving its FSD, the company is breaking new ground in innovation and making huge steps towards changing how we move and connect with the world around us.

Challenges and Controversies of FSD

Tesla's developments in self-driving technology have been absolutely astounding, but they have also drawn major criticism and scrutiny. Accidents involving the company's Autopilot system have sparked controversy over the safety and dependability of self-driving technology. Critics contend that Tesla's advertising of the system's capabilities may lead to misuse, with drivers overestimating its capability and depending on it in ways that endanger safety. The National Highway Traffic Safety Administration (NHTSA) among other regulatory agencies have voiced doubts on the veracity of Tesla's claims on the performance of its FSD capacity. They have also said that efficient operation of these technologies still depends on active driver awareness and involvement.

Getting cars to drive themselves without a person in the driver's seat is mainly a software problem, and Tesla is setting new standards for software solutions. In an interview with the Wall Street Journal in 2022, Elon Musk stressed that this goal needs more than just money; it needs ground-breaking innovative ideas. Musk wants full autonomy to be the foundation of a change in transportation that makes it safer and more efficient. However, making this big dream come true will still be hard and life-changing.

Battery Innovation: The Impact of 4680 Battery Cells

Tesla, led by Elon Musk, introduced its landmark 4680 battery cells in 2020, a paradigm shift with the potential to change the landscape of the electric vehicle (EV) realm. These high-capacity batteries are larger, have a higher power-to-unit ratio, and are less expensive than current geometries, and they allow for Tesla's dream of the world's largest shift to clean energy. The 4680 cells deliver several key advancements:

- ❖ **Enhanced Energy Density:** Batch 4680 battery cells represent a substantial advance in the direction of greater energy storage capacity than all other architectures. It is with this innovation that the range of Tesla vehicles is increased, as well as the relative advantage of Tesla vehicles compared with conventional ICE vehicles. This invention is in line with Elon Musk's idea for true, green, and good electric vehicles to be used every day. Due to their extended range and superior performance, such batteries have finally enabled people to think about EVs as a viable option for daily driving around the world.

- ❖ **Lower Production Costs:** Fueled by unprecedented reengineering of the battery platform and by streamlining manufacturing, Tesla is a reality through the dramatic reduction of production costs. This cost-efficient device enables Tesla to lower the price of its vehicles, making them more accessible and increasing their appeal to a broader audience.

- **Reduced Environmental Impact:** Battery cells of 4680 have a novel electrode architecture capable of significantly reducing cobalt concentration, the compound traditionally closely associated with both poor ethical practices and environmental contamination. With Cobalt use minimized, Tesla overturns the ethical and ecological consequences that are inherent to raw material mining. In addition, the cost of the batteries allowed for the development of them with an energy benefit optimized for greater energy efficiency with a resultant reduced environmental footprint. This change highlights the extra responsibility and sustainability commitments of Tesla as a corporate entity and indicates that the advancement of technologies is not merely advancing technology for its own sake, but it is also shaping us towards a more sustainable tomorrow.

Musk said, "We need to make sure we're doing the right thing, not just for Tesla, but for society as a whole," in 2020 on Tesla's Battery Day, emphasizing the significance of environmental stewardship.

The unwavering commitment to sustainability and innovation that characterizes Elon Musk's leadership at Tesla still impacts sectors and addresses global concerns today. From transforming the electric car market to supporting the deployment of renewable energies, Musk always stands on the fringe of what's achievable. Batteries of the 4680 type are a perfect realization of such a vision.

Tesla's Impact on Manufacturing

Tesla's approach to manufacturing is as revolutionary as its products. Elon Musk calls it "the machine that builds the machine" because its core to the company's mission of accelerating the world's transition to sustainable energy.

By automating everything, Tesla puts robotics and AI on the assembly lines to speed up precision and reduce human error. Streamlined processes eliminate waste, and vertical integration allows Tesla to make batteries for the software in-house. This pushes the boundaries of traditional manufacturing, so Tesla's factories are as futuristic as the cars and tech they produce. The result is a production system that meets demand and sets new standards for efficiency and sustainability.

Tesla's Gigapress is a massive die-casting machine that's one of the company's most important manufacturing innovations, changing how cars are made. Unlike traditional methods, where cars are assembled from hundreds of smaller parts welded or bolted together (a time-consuming and complicated process), the Gigapress makes large single-piece car parts in one cast. This is the philosophy Elon has been preaching for years, "The best part is no part. The best process is no process." The Gigapress is the embodiment of that, simplifying Tesla's manufacturing process and delivering big benefits:

- ❖ **Faster production:** With faster and more efficient manufacturing processes, Tesla can scale up to meet the growing global demand for electric vehicles. By means of innovative methods of production and automation, Tesla can expedite assembly lines, therefore eliminating delays and increasing output. This allows them to produce more vehicles in less time so consumers may acquire their vehicles sooner. This is important as more people are switching to sustainable transportation.

- ❖ **Lower cost:** Simplified and optimized production methods reduce manufacturing costs by eliminating unnecessary complexity, materials, and labor time. Tesla's approach is to design cars that are easier and faster to make, which means lower costs for the company. These savings are passed on to customers, making Tesla vehicles more competitive and affordable to a wider range of consumers. Tesla's dedication to affordability is part of its ambition to hasten the global transition to sustainable energy.

- ❖ **Better durability:** By using fewer parts and simplifying designs, Tesla reduces the number of joints, seams, and weak places in their vehicles. This thoughtful engineering approach means stronger more durable cars that will last longer. Fewer parts also mean less chance of mechanical failures so better reliability over the life of the car. Customers get a better product and reduced maintenance needs and long-term ownership costs so more value from their Tesla.

This is what Musk calls merging of latest technology with practicality, a new standard for the industry. By eliminating thousands of welds and simplifying assembly as he said in a 2021 interview with Automotive News the Gigapress is "a game changer for the industry". It changes how cars are made and pushes the industry towards a more efficient and sustainable future. (Source: Tesla Investor Day Presentation, 2023)

Tesla Energy: Building a Better World

Tesla is now a renewable energy company, not just a car company. It's a global leader in sustainable energy solutions and a pioneer in renewable energy. Tesla offers clean power for homes and businesses with its solar panels, Powerwall energy storage, etc., to change the way power is produced, stored, and consumed. These systems will help people get off the grid, and lower their energy bills and carbon footprint. By combining technology with environmental sustainability, Tesla can make renewable energy accessible and practical for everyone and create a greener, more efficient world.

End of Chapter 3 - Deep Insights: The Later Career of Elon Musk

Chapter 3 - Quotes from Musk

- ❖ "If zeal is worthwhile enough, you do it, even if, odds are, you lose." Elon Musk, TED Talk, 2013.
- ❖ "They treated me as though I didn't know what I was talking about." Elon Musk, 60 Minutes, 2012.
- ❖ "We're not trying to be disruptive just for the sake of it. We are making choices on the basis of what we think is right for humanity's fate." Bloomberg, 2016.
- ❖ "Good ideas are always crazy until they're not." TED Talk, 2013.

Chapter 3 - Interesting Facts

- **Mars Oasis Dream:** At first, Musk aimed to purchase old intercontinental ballistic missile (ICBM) systems from Russia to build a small greenhouse on Mars as part of his "Mars Oasis" dream (Vance, 2015).

- **The Beginnings of SpaceX:** SpaceX started in a modest facility in El Segundo, California, with Musk investing $100 million of his personal fortune to fund the company (Vance, 2015).

- **Falcon 1 Challenges and Triumphs:** The fourth launch of SpaceX's Falcon 1 rocket was a do-or-die situation for SpaceX because it had depleted all its financial resources after three launch failures (Berger, 2018).
    - Successful Falcon 1 orbit in 2008, by SpaceX, first put a privately funded company on that achievement and transformed the face of space travel (SpaceX, 2008).

- **Tesla's Early Financial Struggles:** Tesla once faced bankruptcy during the 2008 financial crisis, and Musk personally funded payroll using his remaining savings from the PayPal sale (Tesla, 2019).

Quirky Tesla Trivia

- The earlier sign of the Tesla logo, "T," is an electric motor cross-section (Tesla, 2016).

- Musk named the Model S, 3, X, and Y to spell "SEXY," though the Model 3 replaced "E" due to trademark issues (Vance, 2015).

- Easter eggs are everywhere—a game-like ability in which the screen becomes a Mario Kart racetrack or the Monty Python classic, Always Look on the Bright Side of Life (Tesla, 2018), plays on a constant loop.

Chapter 3 - Key Points

- ❖ **SpaceX's Vision for Humanity:** Elon Musk's scenario of a multi-planetary human society has driven space travel and Martian society in SpaceX.
- ❖ **Persistence Against Challenges:** Despite near-catastrophic failures and financial challenges, SpaceX's persistence paid off with its historic Falcon 1 success in 2008.
- ❖ **Private Innovation in Space Exploration:** The success of SpaceX not only proved but demonstrated that innovation in one domain could be carried out by private companies, a domain of exclusive government control, and this has profound effects on the future of space exploration.
- ❖ **Tesla's Market Impact:** Tesla changed the landscape of the electric car market by showing that electric cars can be desirable, high-powered, and environmentally friendly.
- ❖ **Risk-Taking and Perseverance:** Musk's persistence and willingness to take risks have been pivotal in overcoming production and financial hurdles.
- ❖ **Beyond Electric Cars:** Tesla's innovations do not stop at cars, but rather they have led to energy storage and solar energy technology innovations.

Chapter 3 - Questions to Ponder

1. How can Musk's approach to "first principles thinking" be implemented to address problems in other areas of industry?
2. What does the success of SpaceX teach us about the role that private actors may play in addressing global-scale problems?
3. What role can resilience and grit under chronic failure play in achieving new and creative insights?
4. How has Musk's vision for Tesla changed over time, and what role did previous experiences play in this change?

5. What can we learn from Tesla's attempt to scale production in the face of challenges?
6. What will be the impact of Tesla's commitment to sustainability on global energy policy?

Chapter 3 - Activities

1. **Tracking SpaceX's Growth**
   Create a timeline of SpaceX's key milestones from its founding in 2002 to its first successful Falcon 1 launch in 2008.

2. **Imagining a Mars Payload**
   Imagine you're tasked with designing a small payload for Musk's original "Mars Oasis" mission. What would you include and why?

3. **Debating Space Exploration**
   Support a debate about whether space exploration should be conducted with the government or the private sector.

4. **Exploring Battery Technology**
   Study the development of lithium-ion batteries as well as their contribution to cost reduction due to Tesla Gigafactories.

5. **Business Model Comparisons**
   Write an essay comparing Tesla's business model with that of a legacy automaker like Ford or GM.

Present Day: Neuralink, The Boring Company, and X

Exploring New Frontiers

Elon Musk's working on some groundbreaking innovations that will change human life. These projects show that Musk has an amazing ability to think outside the box. He keeps using cutting-edge technology and big goals to solve important problems around the world and make people's lives better.

Neuralink: Redefining the Relationship Between Humans and Machines

Neuralink is one of Elon's most audacious and futuristic projects to connect humans to machines. At its core, Neuralink is developing technology to interface directly with the human brain, things that have been science fiction for decades. Musk has said repeatedly Neuralink is not just about human enhancement but about making sure we can keep up with the pace of AI. As he said on the Joe Rogan Experience podcast in 2020: "We're trying to increase the bandwidth between your brain and the digital world. This is about symbiosis with AI."

Neuralink has multiple facets, with the immediate focus on medical and the long term on expanding human capability. Musk has said repeatedly that while the future applications of Neuralink may seem far out, the company's current focus is on solving real medical problems.

Medical Rehabilitation: Transforming Lives

Neuralink is going to revolutionize the treatment of untreatable neurological conditions.

- ❖ **Paralysis:** The company is working on brain-machine interfaces that would allow paralyzed people to control devices like smartphones, computers, or prosthetics with their minds.

Musk has called this technology to restore autonomy and communication for people living with severe physical limitations.

- **Neurodegenerative Diseases:** Parkinson's and Alzheimer's could be mitigated by Neuralink's technology which would strengthen or even reverse the damage caused by these conditions. Musk has said this would improve the quality of life for millions of people worldwide.

Enhancing Cognitive Functions: Expanding Human Potential

Looking further ahead Neuralink will transform how we interact with technology and each other. The possibilities include faster learning, better memory retention and even "telepathic" communication through brain-to-brain interfaces. Musk has said this could one day enable us to process information at the speed of AI and what he calls "a high-bandwidth connection between the brain and the digital world."

In a 2021 interview at The Wall Street Journal CEO Council Summit Musk said Neuralink could lead to downloading skills directly into the brain – what he called "Matrix-style learning". This is decades away, but it shows Musk's belief in humans being able to transcend biological limitations through technology.

Challenges and Ethical Dilemmas

Despite the potential Neuralink has many challenges and ethical questions to consider.

- **Surgical Risks:** Even with Neuralink's robotic precision brain surgeries carry risks – infections, damage to brain tissue or unintended side effects. Musk has acknowledged these risks and said Neuralink will make the procedures as safe as possible.
- **Privacy:** Neuralink's ability to access and store neural data raises questions about data security, consent, and the misuse of

extremely personal information. Musk has said privacy will be "a top priority" for Neuralink.

- ❖ **Economic Inequality:** Critics worry that the latest neural technologies will be only available to the rich, exacerbating existing inequalities. Musk hopes costs will come down and Neuralink will be widely available like Tesla's electric cars.

Elon Musk's Broader Vision for Neuralink

Neuralink is not just an idea; it's Elon's vision for the future—a crazy attempt to save humanity. From turning Tesla into a clean energy company to making a multi-planetary civilization with SpaceX, Elon's companies always push the boundaries of technology no matter how hard it seems.

Neuralink is his attempt to get humanity ready for an AI future. He has said that if you can't beat AI, join it. In a 2020 TED talk he said "If you can't beat AI, join it" which means Neuralink is necessary to preserve human autonomy in an age of rapid technological progress. By building a seamless interface between humans and AI, Neuralink wants to create a future where technology increases human potential not replaces it.

Neuralink has just started but the impact on medicine and human tech interaction is already showing up. The company's core philosophy is that human ingenuity can solve even the biggest problems. This bold mindset is what Neuralink's vision is all about: scaling human intervention to the pace of the world. Musk said in a 2021 Clubhouse conversation that "Neuralink is part of that future". Whether you're skeptical or excited Neuralink applies to many areas, from medicine to tech and to the very nature of being human.

Through Neuralink, Musk urges society to dream beyond its current limitations, envisioning a world where humans and machines integrate seamlessly. This groundbreaking innovation challenges us to imagine a future in which technology not only complements human life but also elevates it.

Starlink: Elon Musk's Vision for a Connected World

Starlink is Elon's big push to solve one of the world's biggest problems: universal internet access. Despite being in the digital age, nearly 3 billion people globally still don't have reliable internet due to geographical isolation, economic barriers, or lack of infrastructure. Elon's vision is to close that gap by using satellite technology to bring high-speed internet to the most remote parts of the planet. By launching thousands of low earth orbit satellites, Starlink is not just about technology – it's about changing the future of connectivity and equality for all.

Starlink's potential to transform lives is already evident across various sectors:

- **Rural and Remote Areas:** Starlink provides high-speed internet to rural and underdeveloped regions that other providers have disregarded. Many people are experiencing their first reliable, fast internet connection, allowing them to access education, business, and the rest of the world.

- **Educational Access:** Schools in remote regions can now access online learning resources, and education is being given in a new way. In a 2023 BBC interview, a teacher from a remote community in Peru said, "For the first time, my students can watch educational videos and connect with the world. It's opening doors we didn't realize existed." These resources don't just improve academic opportunities - they introduce students to new ideas, cultures, and opportunities, giving hope to communities that have endured educational obstacles for generations.

- **Economic Development:** Small businesses in rural areas can now access global markets, sell online, and communicate with customers all over the world. Using e-commerce platforms and digital tools, they can showcase their products to an international audience and overcome geographical barriers. This drives sales, revenue, and local economic growth and creates jobs and innovation in their community.

Musk's vision goes beyond just technology deployment. It's about social transformation through connectivity. In 2020, he said in an interview: "Starlink is designed to connect the unconnected and bring opportunity to the most isolated parts of Earth" (CNBC, 2020).

While challenges like regulations and affordability exist, Starlink's rapid growth and global reach show Musk's commitment to a more connected world. By combining innovation with purpose, Starlink creates a world where no one is left in the dark.

Starlink's Role in Global Crises

- **Ukraine Conflict (2022):** When traditional communications infrastructure was down due to the war, Starlink stepped in to provide connectivity. Through SpaceX's satellite internet service, civilians and government operations can maintain communication, stay informed, and coordinate during crises. Ukrainian officials publicly thanked Musk for this timely intervention, which was critical in areas where ground-based infrastructure was destroyed. (Source: Reuters)

- **Natural Disasters:** Starlink terminals developed under Elon Musk's SpaceX initiative are becoming a lifeline in disaster zones. After the Tonga volcanic eruption and the Haiti earthquake, Starlink's satellites ensured communication for relief efforts when traditional services failed. These deployments show Starlink's ability to deliver fast and reliable internet to remote and devastated areas. (Source: The Verge)

Challenges for Starlink

Elon Musk wants to change the world by launching up to 40,000 satellites through the SpaceX Starlink project and creating a global high-speed internet network. Some challenges:

- **Space Debris Management:** As more satellites go into orbit, space junk is growing into a bigger problem. SpaceX is working on improved deorbiting systems to make sure that satellites are taken out of orbit safely, burn up on re-entry when their time is up, and there is less chance of collisions and debris buildup. Musk has said that the most important thing for this network is that it runs in a way that doesn't add to orbital overcrowding. (From a SpaceX press release in 2023)

- **Regulatory Problems:** Governments and regulatory bodies oppose Starlink because they fear that foreigners may seize control of critical infrastructure. People's perceptions of Starlink are not entirely positive. Some countries consider it a threat to their freedom. To address this, SpaceX is collaborating with foreign authorities to follow the rules and create trust in the markets where the service is expanding. (Reuters. 2023).

Elon Musk's ambitions for Starlink demonstrate his desire to push the boundaries of technology while coping with difficult challenges. If it works, it has the potential to transform the way people communicate and connect all across the world.

The Boring Company: Redefining Urban Landscapes

Cities have been fighting urban congestion for years, and it's led to longer commutes, more pollution, and a lower quality of life. Besides being expensive, traditional solutions harm the environment. Building big public transit systems or widening highways is part of that. Elon Musk founded The Boring Company to solve this problem.

By building underground tunnel networks for high-speed transit, the company will remove congestion, according to the company's mission statement, which is to "bore the future of transportation." These tunnels will be accessible to vehicles equipped with electric sleds, enabling them to travel through them faster and more efficiently than they would be able to do on the surface. Musk says, "Traffic is soul-destroying…It's one of the few things in life that's worse year after year. I'm not going to sit there and do nothing about it" (The Boring Company, 2017). With this approach, Musk and The Boring Company will revolutionize urban transit and change how we think about transportation infrastructure.

The Boring Company is changing the tunnel construction industry with its new tunnel boring machines (TBMs). They are a lot faster and cheaper than the old ones so projects can be done faster and cheaper.

This aligns with Musk's overarching goal of alleviating urban traffic congestion by constructing underground transit networks such as the Hyperloop and reducing the costs associated with infrastructure development. By increasing tunneling efficiency The Boring Company can make it possible for cities around the world to do large underground construction projects.

They do this with two key innovations:

- **Smaller tunnel diameter:** By building tunnels smaller, The Boring Company can waste less material and spend less on excavation. As a result, the expenses associated with tunneling projects are decreased, and the building of more underground networks is made feasible without exceeding the expenditure limits that have been established. This fits Elon's philosophy of using resources efficiently while keeping the end product practical and working.

- **Simultaneously installing tunnel linings:** Unlike traditional TBMs that excavate and then pause to install tunnel linings, The Boring Company's technology allows both to happen simultaneously. Combining these processes can speed up construction time and reduce delays and downtime. This means projects can be completed faster, so underground infrastructure can be built quicker.

TBC's Revolutionary Projects

- **Vegas Loop:** Launched in 2021 by The Boring Company, founded by Elon Musk, the Vegas Loop is a glimpse into the future of urban transportation. This uses Tesla to shuttle people through underground tunnels between key points in Las Vegas, the Convention Center, and resorts. By integrating technology for autonomous vehicles with underground infrastructure, the Vegas Loop will reduce the amount of traffic on the surface and provide a quicker and more efficient transportation method. The Vegas Loop is a real-world example of what can be extended to other cities in the future according to Elon Musk's vision for city mobility, which is currently being implemented (Source: The Boring Company website).

- **Proposed Hyperloop:** Elon Musk's Hyperloop is a game changer for long-distance travel. Pods will travel over 600mph in near vacuum tunnels, which is the most efficient and sustainable way to travel. First proposed in a 2013 white paper, the Hyperloop is being developed by Musk's companies, SpaceX, and The Boring Company. Still in the experimental stage but a big step forward in reimagining the future of travel with speed and environmental consciousness at the core. (Source: SpaceX Hyperloop Alpha White Paper, 2013)

Criticisms and Limitations of The Tunnels

- **Car Dependency:** Elon is too car-centric; his Tesla and the Boring Company's tunnel projects instead of investing in mass transit solutions benefitting more people. For instance, people who support public transport say that putting private cars in underground tubes will only make people more dependent on cars and won't solve city traffic problems in the long run. (Source: The Atlantic, "The Problem with Musk's Tunnel Vision")

- **Feasibility of Expansion:** The Boring Company's initiatives, such as the Vegas Loop, are novel; nonetheless, there are questions over the scalability of these projects in densely populated areas. According to an article published in Wired with the title "Elon Musk's Tunnel Vision Faces Real-World Obstacles," urban planners are cautious about the capability of tunneling technology to overcome the challenges posed by high prices, regulatory impediments, and the difficulty of expanding the system in a metropolitan area with a dense population.

In response to that, he says, "If we don't try radical ideas, we'll never solve the world's biggest problems" (A TED Talk from 2017).

X, formerly known as Twitter

Elon Musk and the Reinvention of Twitter: The Evolution into X

Elon Musk ventured into an uncharted social media area in October 2022. He added another chapter to his already legendary career with the $44 billion acquisition of Twitter, one of the most powerful digital platforms in the world. He believed that technology should be used to improve society, and that free speech should be protected. This wasn't just a business deal; he was making his goal clear.

Musk had more in mind for Twitter than just taking it over. He wanted to make the site known as a spot where everyone could be heard, and he tried to address concerns about censorship and content control. His plan was to transform Twitter into a worldwide public square, a digital area where ideas could flow, and people of all backgrounds could engage.

This fits with his broader mission: to shape the future across multiple areas. From electric cars to space exploration, Musk's companies are about innovation. With Twitter—rebranded as X—he's taking that to communication and digital freedom, to how we exchange ideas and navigate the digital world.

Why Musk Bought Twitter

Elon didn't just buy Twitter for the money; he did it because he was worried about what would happen to free speech, and because he wanted to create a SuperApp. He saw that some points of view were being blocked because of more political bias and blocking on social media. He saw this as a path to centralization, increased societal division, and a decrease in the number of various opinions in a healthy democracy.

For Musk, Twitter served as more than just a social media platform; it served as a virtual forum where individuals could showcase and debate their ideas. By buying Twitter Musk wanted to reverse the trend of control over online discourse and get the platform back to being the unfiltered public square of the digital age. For Musk, the free exchange of ideas wasn't just an idea—it was the foundation of progress and innovation.

A Champion of Free Speech

Musk has always believed in free speech, and it has shaped his choices and public comments. As he said before:

"Free speech is the foundation of a functioning democracy and Twitter is the digital town square where the issues of the world are debated" (KTVU, 2022).

This belief was one of the reasons he bought Twitter and for the massive changes he made when he took over the platform. He didn't want to own a social media company but to turn it into a place where trust could be restored through transparency and open conversation. He wanted a platform where all voices—regardless of popularity or controversy—could have a say in the conversation without being censored. Musk prioritized fairness, transparency and no censorship, a break from the practices many critics believed were stifling free speech (Al Jazeera, 2023).

For Musk, making X better was secondary to preserving a fundamental democratic principle in the digital age. He saw X as a tool to empower individuals and the debates that shape the future of humanity. In Musk's mind, X could be a beacon of free speech in a polarized and digitally driven world.

The Challenges Ahead

Big visions come with big challenges and Musk's plans for X are no exception. His plan to change the platform is full of complexities as he's trying to solve some of the biggest and longest-standing problems in social media. Those problems include:

- It has always been hard for social media sites to deal with fake news while also encouraging real, important conversations. Misinformation breaks trust, leads people astray, and gets in the way of honest conversation. Musk wants to find a way for people to have talks that are well-informed, open, and honest, without any deception or manipulation.

- Getting rid of bots and spam that clog timelines and erode user trust. In recent years, bots have become an obstacle to real user interaction, often posting irrelevant or harmful content. Musk wants a platform where users can have an engaging, authentic environment free of spam and automated malicious accounts.

- Balancing safety, inclusivity, and free expression is difficult. A balanced approach is needed to protect people from harm and encourage free speech. Musk wants a platform that supports free expression, meaningful interaction, and diverse viewpoints. He hopes to provide a platform where people can openly share their opinions without fear of harm or abuse.

These are big goals and critical to the problems of social media platforms, so Musk's plan for X is one of the most watched in the tech world. Musk's vision requires more than just technical breakthroughs—it requires social and ethical understanding. Still, Musk is relentless despite those difficulties. He thinks X has massive potential.

Rebranding Twitter to X

Elon Musk's redesign of Twitter as X was one of his most audacious and symbolic ventures. His objective was not just to brand the platform; he wanted to turn it into a complex digital ecosystem.

In rebranding, Musk plays on his obsession with the letter X, a symbol that has shown up many times in his work. From SpaceX to X.com—the forerunner to PayPal—and Tesla's Model X, the letter stands for Musk's faith in innovation, boundless potential, and challenging norms. Musk himself has stated that the letter X represents the future and his willingness to launch new companies that disrupt the present situation. By rebranding Twitter as X, he expressed his intention to push the platform's capabilities (The Guardian, 2023).

Expanding Beyond Microblogging

Renaming Twitter as X also means transcending microblogging. By adding fresh features and establishing a free space for all interactions, Musk aims to transform our participation in the digital sphere. He wants X to be a major participant in technology, influence how companies and individuals interact, transform the nature of business in the twenty-first century, and so shape society.

As a leader in the digital world, Musk has spent his whole career pushing the limits and questioning what is already known. Now is his chance to prove himself. He is now making X the base of the digital world by connecting imagination, usefulness, and connectivity in ways that have never been seen before.

Musk's Changes to X: Innovation Meets Controversy

Elon Musk's radical improvements to X (previously known as Twitter) have reshaped the platform, reflecting his ambitious vision of innovation and disruption while eliciting strong criticism. He's also changed some core features, such as the verification system and content moderation policies, and many users and experts are questioning the safety of the platform and the spread of truth. This has more significant effects on the platform's global reach, its ability to deal with bad content, and its ability to stay alive in a crowded social media space in the long run.

Layoffs and Operational Changes

One of Musk's first acts as CEO was to lay off almost 75% of the X workforce, a move he justified as necessary to improve efficiency and ensure the company's long-term survival. He stated that a smaller workforce would decrease bureaucracy, save operational expenses, and foster creativity and agility. In a 2022 all-hands meeting, he stated, "The company needs to be efficient and sustainable." While it was criticized for impacting staff and workplace morale, Musk defended it as a necessary step to streamline the company and position X for future growth in a competitive marketplace.

But this massive reduction in staff created problems for the platform and users:

- **Technical Issues:** Outages and platform instability became frequent as the more minor team struggled to manage X's complex infrastructure. With fewer engineers, routine maintenance and bug fixing became impossible and users experienced downtime.

- **Slower Support:** Users got slower responses to customer support and many reported issues were left unsolved or ignored. This lack of timely support left users angry and eroded trust in the platform's ability to fix their problems.

- **Expertise Gone:** The departure of key teams like trust and safety meant the platform couldn't handle bad stuff. Critics said this was a major reason for the rise in misinformation, harassment and other forms of toxicity and a less safe space for users.

X Premium and Revenue Diversification

Musk introduced X Premium, a subscription-based model to reduce the platform's ad dependency and have a more consistent revenue stream. This aligns with Musk's goal of a self-sustaining platform and more benefits to subscribers.

- **For Subscribers**: Paid users receive numerous benefits and coveted verified checkmarks, enhancing their credibility and trust. Subscribers get priority in visibility, so their content shows up more on timelines and in search. They also get access to post editing, tweet undo and advanced customization options, more convenience and flexibility.

- **Goal of Combatting Bots:** Musk claims that charging payment for these functions is a means to battle bots and fraudulent accounts. The purpose of implementing a paywall is to make it more difficult for inauthentic accounts to flood the network, resulting in a more genuine and engaging experience for users. However, the outcomes are mixed:

- **Adoption Rates:** Some users have switched to X Premium because they like the extra tools and visibility. However, critics say the model divides people because it makes free users feel like their material is less important than that of paid subscribers. This has made people worry about how fair and open the site is.

- **Bot Problem Still Persistent:** No matter what Musk says, the problem with bots and fake accounts still exists. A lot of users say that bad people have found ways to get around the new rules so they can still interrupt real talks. A lot of people think that paywalls aren't enough to stop bots.

X Premium shows Musk's plans for how to make money from the platform and fix problems that have been going on for a long time. But we still don't know what the long-term effects will be on the app and how users interact with it.

Content Moderation and Algorithm Transparency

Musk prioritized transparency and user empowerment in reimagining X's content moderation and algorithms.

- **Open-Source Algorithms**
  Musk made X's algorithms open source so users can see how content is ranked, flagged, and recommended on the platform. This gives users and developers a better understanding of how content is visible, and decisions are made on the platform. Musk called this "building trust" with the user base and said it's part of his vision for open digital platforms. By making this info public X hopes to get feedback and collaboration to improve the algorithms continually.

- **Decentralized Moderation**
  From a one-size-fits-all content moderation policy X now enables users tailor their own content choices. This function is meant to provide every user a more customized experience so they may choose what material they interact with and view. People who support free speech and personal freedom are happy about this, but it has also been strongly criticized.

Concerns

- **Enabling Harmful Content:** Because there is no longer any oversight, Musk has made it easier for harassment, hate speech, and false information to spread. Critics say this decentralized approach leaves vulnerable users exposed to bad behavior.

- **Accountability:** With users in control of their feeds how will the platform deal with false information or offensive content when moderation is no longer centralized?

Musk says this is part of his vision for a more open internet, but others say it will undermine a safe and trustworthy digital space.

The Blocking System Overhaul: A Safety Concern

One of the biggest changes on the platform is the blocking system. Users used to rely on blocking as a vital tool to protect themselves from harassment, abuse, and stalking, having control over their online experience. But Musk's decision to limit this feature has everyone concerned, leaving many feeling unsafe and more exposed to bad interactions.

- **Impact on User Safety:** Women, LGBTQ+ people, and activists among vulnerable users worry they will be more likely to be harassed and abused. Many found that blocking undesired interactions served as a safety net; however, this safety net has been taken away and begs serious concerns about their safety on the site.

- **Community Reaction:** The blocking changes have been met with backlash from users, advocacy groups and even cybersecurity experts. Many say it's all about engagement metrics (views and interactions) over user safety. Critics say this will alienate users who value a safe and respectful online space and will hurt the platform's long-term reputation. Many users have looked for an alternative place to call "home" after feeling uncomfortable on X after the changes Musk put into place.

- According to NBC News, 75 out of the top 100 US advertisers have left X since October 2022. The number of active daily users worldwide has also dropped by 15% between February 2022 (before Musk) and February 2023.
- Mvemnt and NBC News noted that this year many users have jumped from using Twitter to other alternatives like Threads (by Meta) or BlueSky (run by the people who originally created Twitter) as Mvemnt states that when Musk promised a platform for free speech what users got instead was a surge of hate speech, misinformation, and "straight-up chaos".

As online safety becomes a bigger topic, this change has brought up the question of balance between user engagement and protecting individuals from bad behavior.

Effects on Elections and Global Impact

Musk's changes to X's AI systems and the relaxation of content moderation have had a significant impact on elections and global politics.

- **Role in Misinformation:** X has been directly involved in spreading false narratives, propaganda, and manipulated information during election periods. This has undermined democracy by shaping public opinion based on misinformation or made-up content. The platform's use of AI to boost engagement has often amplified harmful misinformation, making it hard for users to know what's real and what's not.
- **Global Impact:** In Brazil, X was temporarily banned due to spreading misinformation during an election, which threatened to disrupt the democratic process, and Musk refusing to deal with it. This exposed the enormity of the challenge of global content management and questioned the platform's commitment to ethical content moderation. Similar problems have surfaced in other nations where X has come under fire for not doing enough to combat controversial content and bot tricks used in elections.

Decline in Trustworthiness

While Musk's citizen journalism push is supposed to democratize information and give everyone a voice, the lack of fact-checking is turning X into a misinformation breeding ground. Without clear standards or oversight, X can't be seen as a trusted source of news. The erosion of journalistic standards has been made worse by the platform prioritizing engagement over accuracy, so sensationalism is winning over truth.

These changes haven't just affected election outcomes but have also eroded trust in digital platforms as a whole, so what's the role and responsibility of social media in upholding democratic values globally?

Promoting Citizen Journalism

Elon Musk has been a big supporter of independent creators, and he launched the Monetization for Creators program. People who use this program to make and share content on the site can get paid directly by supporters. By giving creators financial incentives, he's trying to break the monopoly of traditional media and promote diverse grassroots perspectives.

- **Pros:** This allows creators to create unique content, amplify voices that would otherwise be silent. It also promotes more narratives and a more prosperous and more diverse information landscape.

- **Cons:** But without robust and effective moderation in place, there's a risk of misinformation or harmful content spreading under the guise of independent journalism. Balancing free speech with content oversight is a big challenge.

Democratizing Information

Musk wants X to be a place where all views can coexist, regardless of background or affiliation. His goal is to create an open platform that decentralizes information and gets rid of the traditional gatekeepers. That's in line with the broader mission of making information available to everyone.

However, critics argue that making all content equal—verified or not—can make it hard for users to tell facts from opinions. So, the platform's credibility will suffer if unverified or misleading content takes off. Balancing high-quality information with a democratic exchange of ideas is a tough act for X.

Balancing Innovation and Controversy

Musk is reshaping X big time, but it's a high-risk experiment. He's added new features and revenue streams but also user safety, misinformation and global implications. As he continues to remake X, the future of the platform will depend on finding the balance between innovation and accountability.

The Super App Dream

Inspired by multifunctional platforms like WeChat in China, Elon Musk has said X will become a "super app" all-in-one digital hub that combines many functions. From messaging and social networking to payments, shopping and more, the goal is to create a platform so versatile and comprehensive that it becomes essential in the digital age. This is a big ask and will redefine how we interact with technology and have access to multiple services in one app.

In an interview with The Verge, he stated that "If done right, X can be the most useful app in the world where people can connect, transact, and share ideas freely and securely" (The Verge, 2023).

This includes combining advanced financial tools, AI features, and improved communication capabilities to transform X into a hub for commerce, innovation, and social engagement (CNBC, 2023).

1. **Communication**

    - **Enhanced Messaging:** X will add encrypted chats and dynamic conversation threads. Musk wants X to be like WhatsApp.

    - **Voice and Video:** X could be the central hub for personal and professional communication and compete with Zoom and Microsoft Teams (Reuters, 2023)

2. **Transactions**
   - **Integrated Payments:** Users will be able to send money instantly for tasks like bill splitting, tipping creators or paying freelancers (like Venmo or PayPal).
   - **Commerce Support:** Businesses on X will have secure and efficient payment solutions to do direct transactions without needing external payment platforms. Musk has said reducing friction in digital payments is key to adoption (TechCrunch, 2023).

3. **Shopping**
   - **E-commerce Capabilities:** It will be possible for companies and creators to establish virtual storefronts within X, transforming it into a marketplace like Shopify or Instagram Shopping, respectively.
   - **Streamlined Experiences**: Users will be able to browse, buy and track their orders all within the app and never leave.

4. **Content Creation and Sharing**
   - **Empowering Creators:** X will give creators the tools to publish articles, stream videos and monetize their work. The aim is to create a creator economy that rewards innovation and engagement.
   - **Analytics and Insights:** Built-in analytics will let creators see their audience, and refine their growth and influence strategy (CNBC, 2023)

Overall Goals for X

When it comes to making life simpler, more connected, and more creative, Musk's X will be all about seamless integration, which means mixing a wide variety of features and services into a single platform.

By combining communication, transactions, and e-commerce into one app, you'll save time and not have to manage multiple tools and platforms. Musk says we need to "get rid of unnecessary complexity in daily digital interactions" (Business Insider, 2023).

X will bridge the gap between social and functional interactions, deeper relationships, and productivity. X is for personal connection and professional collaboration. Creators will have advanced tools to express themselves. Live streaming and AI content personalization will be the canvas. (Wired, 2023)

Whether you're chatting with friends, running a business or exploring new content X will have what you need in one place.

Musk's X is all about innovation and forward thinking, solving today's problems while anticipating tomorrow's user needs. Using AI, X will offer personalized recommendations, predictive tools and automated workflows that adapt to user behavior (CNBC, 2023). X will have blockchain for secure payments, AR for shopping and AI-driven content creation (Wired, 2023). X will be a global platform, bridging the digital divide and inclusion even in areas with no connectivity (Business Insider, 2023).

Musk has said X will be "the most useful thing in the world" (The Verge, 2023). The journey to get there will be hard and complicated but that's just Musk being ambitious as always.

If it becomes successful X will transform the digital world and establish the standard for how platforms may unite all of life into one place. Whether X gets there or not it's a big step towards a new kind of digital.

The Road Ahead

There are challenges ahead – user adoption and technological implementation – but Musk's vision puts X at the forefront of reimagining digital experiences.

- **Balancing Innovation and Usability:** Achieving success will depend on creating a platform that combines bold technological advancements with user-centric design (Wired, 2023).

- **Setting New Paradigms:** If successful, X won't just redefine digital experiences; it will establish new paradigms for how people work, play, and connect in the years to come (Forbes, 2023).

Musk's vision for X is classic Musk – he loves to disrupt and push boundaries. If this works, X will be a game changer, shaping the future of human interaction and the digital world.

End of Chapter 4 - Deep Insights: Present Day: Neuralink, The Boring Company, and X

Chapter 4 - Quotes from Musk

- ❖ "Traffic is soul-destroying. It's one of the few things in life that's worse year after year. I'm not going to sit there and do nothing about it." (The Boring Company, 2017)

- ❖ "We're trying to increase the bandwidth between your brain and the digital world. This is about symbiosis with AI." (Joe Rogan Experience, 2020)

- ❖ "Free speech is the bedrock of a functioning democracy, and Twitter is the digital town square where matters vital to the future of humanity are debated."

- ❖ "Starlink is designed to connect the unconnected and bring opportunity to the most isolated parts of Earth." (CNBC, 2020)

- ❖ "If we don't try radical ideas, we'll never solve the world's biggest problems." (TED Talk, 2017)

- ❖ "AI is a rare case where we need to be proactive in regulation rather than reactive. Because if we're reactive in AI regulation, it's too late." (National Governors Association, 2017)

Chapter 4 - Interesting Facts

- ❖ Neuralink's brain-machine interfaces could allow paralyzed people to control devices like smartphones and prosthetics with their minds, making it an accessibility game-changer.

- ❖ The Boring Company is using simultaneous tunnel lining during excavation to cut project timelines and costs in half.

- Starlink has provided internet to disaster zones, Tonga after the volcano erupted and Haiti after the earthquake, so it can work in emergency response.

- X is a "super app" like WeChat, integrating social media, payments, e-commerce, and AI services into one app.

- Neuralink's future applications could be cognitive enhancement, memory retention and even brain-to-brain communication (aka telepathy).

Chapter 4 - Key Points
Neuralink:

- Merging human brains with machines to stay ahead of AI.

- Medical applications first (paralysis, neurodegenerative diseases) and then cognitive enhancements.

- Ethical dilemmas around privacy, accessibility, and brain surgery.

The Boring Company:

- Solving urban congestion with underground high-speed transit.

- Vegas Loop is a proof of concept for urban transformation.

- Tunneling innovations reduce costs and make it more feasible to do.

Starlink:

- Connects the worldwide digital divide by providing high-speed internet to rural and underserved areas.

- Plays a vital role in global crises, providing connectivity in conflict zones and disaster areas.

- Challenges include regulatory opposition and handling space debris from its extensive satellite network.

X:

- Formerly Twitter, it's becoming a digital ecosystem for communication, transactions and creative expression.

- Launched X Premium to diversify revenue and fight bots.

- Promoting transparency and decentralized content moderation to rebuild trust and open conversation.

Chapter 4 – Questions to Ponder

1. What are the ethical considerations for Neuralink when developing brain-machine interfaces?
2. How can The Boring Company's tunneling solve urban congestion globally?
3. How can Starlink's global internet bring economic development to remote areas?
4. Do you think X will be a super app? Why or why not?
5. How can Musk balance free speech with fighting misinformation and bad content on X?

Chapter 4 – Activities

1. Analyze Neuralink's impact on medical rehab and human cognition.

2. Debate The Boring Company's urban transportation vision for megacities.
3. Case study: how Starlink has improved life for a rural or disaster-affected community.
4. Brainstorm features for X to be a super app.
5. Essay: the politics and society of Musk's projects and their impact on global innovation and governance.

Present Day: Politics and Family Life

Musk's Approach to Politics: A Pragmatic Visionary

Musk's long-term view of humanity drives his political curiosity. Instead of endorsing a particular philosophy, he advocates practical solutions to present world problems.

Musk has long been an advocate for sustainable living and green energy. Because of how he led Tesla, countries all over the world have made standards about emissions that are stricter and invested more in clean energy.

In 2022, he said, "We need to get to a sustainable energy economy as fast as possible. The sooner the better for the planet and humanity" (CNBC, 2022). His focus on renewable energy has driven Tesla's innovations from electric cars to solar and battery storage.

Governments around the world have noticed Tesla's success and have introduced subsidies and incentives for electric vehicles (EVs) and renewable energy projects. This is not only a reflection of Musk's influence on public policy but also a global effort to reduce carbon and combat climate change (The Guardian, 2023). Through this, he and Tesla are helping to speed up the world to a more sustainable future.

Musk's buying of Twitter (now X) shows that he thinks free speech is important for a democracy. He's been critical of censorship and has emphasized transparency in content moderation.

In 2022, he tweeted, "A platform must allow all voices even those we disagree with. Transparency and neutrality are key" (Twitter, 2022). This is his idea of an open space. Since then, at X, he's open-sourced the algorithms so users and developers can see how content is prioritized and moderated. He's also decentralized moderation, so it's no longer controlled by a single entity to have a more balanced and diverse conversation. This is to address bias and censorship, so the platform remains a space for free speech and fair interaction (TechCrunch, 2023).

Through SpaceX, Musk has changed the game for space exploration. His work with NASA and other governments is an example of public-private collaboration to achieve important things, like reusable rockets and Mars colonization.

NASA Administrator Bill Nelson recently said Elon Musk and SpaceX are key to the future of space exploration. "Elon Musk and SpaceX are essential to America's leadership in space," he said. (NASA, 2023)

A Focus on Problem-Solving

Musk's politics is about solving global problems. His approach is pragmatic not ideological. Musk never aligns himself with any party. He says we should focus on real-world problems not politics. He has often said, "I'm not a fan of politics. I'm focused on solving problems that matter for humanity's future" (Forbes, 2021). The fact that he is not distracted by politics allows him to concentrate on innovation and practical solutions, whether they pertain to sustainable transportation, space exploration, or renewable energy.

Musk believes technology can drive change faster than policy. His companies set the bar for what governments and industries can achieve. As reported by Bloomberg (2023), Tesla's leadership in EV has triggered a global competition among automakers to adopt cleaner technologies and governments to build infrastructure and incentives to support this transition.

Criticism and Support

Musk's political involvement has brought both praise and criticism, as he is a polarizing figure in global conversations.

Critics say Musk's opinions and actions overshadow his ability to stay neutral on big issues. His frequent and sometimes controversial tweets have led some to question his impact on the public discourse and its consequences. For example, his involvement on Twitter where he shares unfiltered thoughts, has raised questions about whether people with big followings have too much power over public opinion and the narrative (The New York Times, 2023). Some worry his influence goes beyond tech and shapes societal debates in ways that aren't always good or balanced.

People from all over the world talk to him about important things like space, artificial intelligence, and green energy. His fans love how he doesn't hide his desire for progress. A lot of people see him as a thought leader who challenges the status quo and does things in a new way.

His actions show how individuals can make a substantial impact on society by bridging the gap between innovation and policy. Musk has consistently shown how entrepreneurship can solve some of the world's biggest problems (Business Insider, 2023).

Elon Musk's politics are part of his overall pursuit for a better future. His method demonstrates that creativity is the driving force behind progress and that leadership can transcend borders and transform the world.

Elon Musk's Stance on AI Regulation: Balancing Innovation and Safety

Elon Musk has long been a vocal advocate for regulating artificial intelligence (AI). While Musk is an ardent proponent of technological advancement, he is equally mindful of the potential risks posed by unchecked AI development. His approach is grounded in a genuine concern for humanity's safety, blending urgency with pragmatism to push for proactive measures that balance innovation with responsibility.

Musk sees AI as a game changer that can solve all of humanity's biggest problems – healthcare, education, climate change, etc. But he also sees the existential risks of uncontrolled AI.

He famously said, "We're summoning the demon" at a 2014 MIT symposium. He's been warning about the dangers of AI if left uncontrolled for years and is advocating for regulation and ethical considerations to make it safe and responsible.

In a 2014 interview, he said, "We need to be very careful with AI. It's more dangerous than nukes." He was drawing a comparison to one of humanity's most destructive creations. He's saying we need to be careful and responsible with AI or we could lose control. This is the duality of Musk's view – AI is a game changer, but if developed irresponsibly, it could be beyond human control.

Unlike many tech leaders who fight regulation, Musk has been advocating for proactive AI governance. His argument is that regulation must come before, not after, the advanced AI capabilities.

At the 2017 National Governors Association meeting, Elon Musk gave a dire warning about AI, telling policymakers to act now. He said, "AI is the only case where we need to be proactive in regulation rather than reactive. Because if we're reactive in AI regulation, it's too late." He said governments need to understand the risks and regulate early so AI doesn't advance unchecked and gets out of control. (CNBC, 2017)

Researchers, government officials, and business leaders should work together, according to Musk, to make rules that will keep AI growth safe, moral, and helpful for everyone.

Tesla's AI Systems

Tesla's autonomous systems are all about AI and show how AI can make transportation safer and more efficient. Musk wants clear safety standards and transparency in these systems to prevent accidents and misuse.

It was in 2022 that Elon Musk said, "Autonomy will save lives, cut down on accidents, and change the way we think about transportation." "But it needs to be done right." He said that the most important thing is to do it in an honest and careful way. The real benefits of autonomy can only be reached through tests, safety rules, and innovative ideas that put people first (Tesla, 2022).

Smart Regulation

Musk proposes frameworks that:

- Promote transparency in AI algorithms.
- Mandate ethical considerations in AI deployment.

- Encourage collaboration between governments, academia, and the private sector (Brookings, 2021).

Musk asserts that the control of AI must transcend national boundaries. The borderless character of AI's influence cannot be addressed without cooperative worldwide efforts.

In 2023, Elon Musk emphasized that the problems posed by artificial intelligence require global attention. As he put it, "AI is a global challenge, and solving it requires international cooperation." He emphasized the necessity of nations cooperating to ensure responsible development and control of AI technology. Financial Times, 2023.

Critics and Supporters of Musk's Stance

Some say Elon Musk's warnings about AI are alarmist and will slow down innovation or scare the public. Musk has repeatedly said the uncontrolled development of AI is as bad as nukes. But skeptics say that's just scaremongering and will stifle progress in the field or overshadow the benefits of AI.

Also, others point out conflicts of interest since Musk is developing AI through Tesla and Neuralink and is also a vocal advocate for AI regulation. He's a tech entrepreneur and an AI regulator. That's a tough narrative to square.

Like this 2022 Atlantic piece: "Musk's dual role as an advocate for regulation and a tech entrepreneur is a conflict of interest that needs to be examined." This dual role has raised questions about whether Musk's agenda is driven by humanity or by self-interest to shape the AI industry to benefit his own companies.

Supporters of Musk's position praise him for putting long-term safety over short-term profit. Many see his calls for regulation as the only way to mitigate risk.

AI ethicist Timnit Gebru said: "Musk's advocacy for AI governance shows we need leadership in an area that will define humanity's future" (MIT Technology Review, 2022). She emphasized the growing relevance of ethics as AI becomes more integrated into our daily lives, from decision-making to infrastructure.

Musk's views on AI legislation demonstrate his willingness to balance innovation and safety. He seeks to ensure that AI is used for good by advocating for regulation, transparency, and ethical AI through OpenAI, Neuralink, and Tesla. His leadership in this area walks a tight line between using AI and safeguarding humans from it.

Working with Governments on AI Regulation

Elon Musk has been a vocal advocate for global cooperation on AI regulation. He knows the incredible opportunities AI presents to revolutionize industries and improve lives and the existential risks if left unchecked. By working with governments and international organizations he wants to create policies that balance innovation with responsibility and prevent the misuse or unintended consequences of advanced AI systems.

Musk's warnings about AI risks have sparked policy discussions on ethical guidelines and international agreements for AI development. He's compared AI regulation to nuclear arms treaties and says we need collective action. At the 2023 AI summit, he said: "We need to work together, across borders and industries, to make sure AI is a tool for good and not a weapon of mass destruction." (Financial Times, 2023)

Musk has proposed the AI Safety Act, an international treaty designed to regulate advanced AI. Still just an idea, it shows Musk is ahead of the curve on AI's global challenges and his broader vision for AI to be aligned with human values.

Driving Renewable Energy Legislation

Elon Musk through Tesla and SolarCity has been driving renewable energy adoption and shaping policy at the national and international level. By innovation and scale, he has made renewable energy a viable alternative to fossil fuels and has influenced the policy agenda on sustainability. Tesla's EVs and solar products have changed the public perception, and governments are now setting more aggressive carbon reduction targets and renewable energy targets.

Advocacy for Carbon Pricing

Musk has always been a big advocate for carbon pricing as the solution to climate change. According to him, energy production would be dominated by renewables if the market reflected the full cost of carbon. In an interview in 2020, he stated:

"If the true cost of carbon were reflected in the market, renewables would dominate energy production." (CNBC, 2020)

Musk's advocacy goes beyond words. Tesla is actively involved in policy discussions and works with environmental groups to push for carbon pricing at local, national, and international level. The company's annual impact reports highlight the importance of decarbonization and call for transparent carbon accounting frameworks. By pricing carbon internally at Tesla, Musk is showing how businesses can lead by example and encourage lawmakers to do the same.

As a carbon pricing advocate, Musk has been saying for years that it's important to put a price on carbon. At the 2021 COP26 conference, he said: *"The real cost of carbon must be reflected in the market to drive meaningful change."* (UN Climate Change, 2021).

His call for economic mechanisms like carbon taxes has been heard by policymakers around the world and is influencing global climate policy and carbon accountability.

Policy Collaboration in Energy Storage

Tesla's large-scale battery projects, including the Hornsdale Power Reserve in Australia, have set the global benchmark for energy storage. These projects have shown how battery technology can stabilize the grid and governments are now introducing subsidies and incentives for renewable energy storage (Reuters, 2021). Hornsdale's success has spawned projects like the Victorian Big Battery and energy storage facilities in California and Texas and a wave of policy action on grid resilience and renewable integration.

Tesla's energy team works closely with utilities and regulatory bodies to shape energy storage policy so that large-scale batteries can plug in to the existing grid. Musk's push for decentralized energy grids, through home-based Powerwalls and community-scale Powerpacks, is also influencing policy on distributed energy resources (DERs) and microgrids.

Impact on Autonomous Transportation Policies

Work on autonomous vehicle (AV) technology by Tesla has spurred legislative activity in this area. Musk's advocacy of Full Self-Driving (FSD) has compelled governments to handle ethical, safety, and liability concerns related to AV applications.

Musk advocates for a collaborative framework to establish common AV guidelines so innovation can happen while public safety is prioritized (Bloomberg, 2022). Working with the National Highway Traffic Safety Administration (NHTSA) and European officials has led to policy changes that happen repeatedly as AV technology gets better. Musk is helping lawmakers make rules based on facts by sharing information from Tesla's real-world driving miles. This balances technological progress with safety standards.

Tesla has ethical decision-making in its AI, as per Musk's overall human-centric AI policies. His emphasis on ethical AI is for responsible technology deployment across industries. Tesla's internal AI teams are working on minimizing algorithmic bias and transparency, so they are a leader in ethical AV development.

Regulatory Clashes

Musk's battles with regulators show the tension between innovation and oversight. His opposition to California's strict AV testing requirements sparked debate on public safety and technological progress (TechCrunch, 2023). Tesla moving production and testing to states with looser regulations is the broader fight between innovators and regulators in uncharted territory.

Satellite Management Issues

Starlink's fast satellite deployment is causing orbital congestion and space debris. Musk acknowledges the issues and promises to fix them, but critics say deployment is outpacing regulations (Nature, 2023). Musk is proposing international cooperation on satellite traffic management, calling for stricter debris mitigation and participating in UN discussions on sustainable space.

Elon Musk's Influence on International Organizations

Elon Musk's ideas and companies go beyond borders, making him a key figure in global policy and strategy. Through SpaceX, Tesla and renewable energy, Musk has worked with the United Nations (UN), the European Union (EU) and the World Economic Forum (WEF). His projects have sparked conversations on space, sustainability, AI and energy and shaped global decision-making.

Space Exploration and Global Cooperation

Elon Musk's view of space goes beyond technology; it's about international cooperation to ensure space is used sustainably and ethically. Through partnerships and dialogues with global bodies, Musk has helped shape the future of space while tackling the big issues.

Collaboration with United Nations Office for Outer Space Affairs (UNOOSA)

Musk's goal of making humanity a multiplanetary species aligns with UNOOSA's mission to promote the peaceful and sustainable use of space. His Mars colonization vision has sparked global conversations on the ethics and logistics of interplanetary settlement.

Space Debris Mitigation

The rapid rollout of SpaceX's Starlink satellite constellation has put orbital debris in the spotlight. Musk has worked with UNOOSA to address this issue, proposing de-orbiting technology and responsible satellite design.

In a 2021 interview, he said, "If we don't act responsibly, space will become a graveyard. Collaboration is key to a sustainable future in orbit." (Nature, 2021)

He has contributed to the global conversation on setting standards for space debris management and the long-term sustainability of orbital activity.

International Space Collaboration

Musk's innovations, especially SpaceX's reusable rockets, have changed the space game. By reducing launch costs so much, SpaceX has made space accessible to smaller countries and space programs.

- **Partnerships with NASA and ESA**
  NASA and ESA partnerships with SpaceX show how public-private partnerships can get important things done. These collaborations, from supporting the International Space Station (ISS) to future Mars expeditions, demonstrate what is possible when we work together (NASA, 2022).

- **Democratizing Space Access**
  Countries without established space programs can conduct scientific research, install satellites, and educate with SpaceX's economical launch services. This is what we call global participation in space exploration and utilization.

Musk's work in space shows us the importance of global cooperation, ethics, and innovation. By working with UNOOSA and partnering with top space agencies, Musk has not only taken humanity further into space but also shown us we need to share the space.

Tesla and the European Green Deal

Tesla has been driving the European Union's Green Deal, which aims to be carbon neutral by 2050. The company's work on electric vehicles

(EVs) and renewable energy has not only accelerated Europe's transition to sustainability but also policy changes and technology.

Tesla's Gigafactory in Berlin is a flagship investment in the European EV market. By increasing EV production, creating thousands of jobs, and driving innovation, the factory is the embodiment of sustainable development. At the factory launch, Musk said: "This is not just a factory – it's a blueprint for sustainable manufacturing." (BBC, 2022).

The factory also shows Tesla's alignment with the EU's goals to electrify transport and reduce greenhouse gas emissions. Musk's work has influenced EU policies on EV infrastructure and renewable energy subsidies. These policies fit with the overall European goal of reducing carbon and integrating clean energy.

Tesla's battery technology advancements – energy density and cost efficiency – have set the global standard. This has pushed European policymakers to put energy storage in their climate strategies and to scale energy innovation (Reuters, 2023).

Musk has been a long-time supporter of IRENA's mission to accelerate the world's transition to renewable energy and has helped make substantial progress in the field.

Tesla's Solar Roof and large battery installations have set new world records for renewable energy integration. Big projects in Australia and Puerto Rico show that it's possible to go all in on clean energy at both residential and utility scale.

IRENA has recognized these as innovation examples (IRENA, 2023).

AI Safety and International Collaboration

Musk's presence at WEF has brought to light the benefits and risks of AI.

Musk wants a WEF-led global task force to create ethical guidelines and regulations for AI. During a 2023 WEF session, he emphasized: *"AI is a double-edged sword. We need to ensure the blade cuts in the direction of progress, not destruction."* (World Economic Forum, 2023). His push for international collaboration aims to address concerns around AI misuse while ensuring its benefits are harnessed responsibly.

Elon Musk's work on the European Green Deal and global AI safety is part of his broader vision to put technology into sustainable development. From revolutionizing EV manufacturing to advocating for responsible AI governance, Musk is shaping policies and strategies for a sustainable and tech advanced future.

Broader Policy Influence

- **Renewable Energy Incentives**
  Musk's work has inspired governments to introduce policies to support renewable energy infrastructure, including subsidies, tax incentives and streamlined regulations for clean energy projects.

- **Battery Technology Leadership**
  Tesla's battery technology has set the global standard, so countries are now prioritizing energy storage as part of their climate strategies. The focus on efficiency and scalability has further reinforced the role of technology in energy independence.

By influencing international organizations, governments and climate forums, Musk has become a leading figure in the fight against climate change and is bringing us closer to a carbon-neutral world.

Strategies for Overcoming Regulatory Hurdles

Elon Musk has made a career out of navigating complex regulatory environments. By combining diplomacy, public engagement, and technology, he has tackled regulatory hurdles while achieving his big goals.

- **Diplomacy and Negotiation**

- Musk has shown a strategic approach to dealing with governments and regulatory bodies, often framing it as a win-win.

- **Gigafactory Berlin Approval**
  - Getting approval for the Tesla Berlin Gigafactory required Musk to navigate EU environmental regulations. He pointed out how the factory aligned with Europe's sustainability goals and would create thousands of jobs. By framing it as a mutual benefit he showed a diplomatic approach that balances innovation and compliance.

- **Public Advocacy**
  - Musk uses his social media presence, particularly X (formerly Twitter), to speak directly to the public and build grassroots support for his projects.

- **Regulatory Transparency**
  - By talking about regulatory issues on social media, Musk not only educates but also mobilizes public opinion to force policymakers to pass good laws. He can get a lot of people on his side which shows the power of public advocacy to get past the bureaucracy.

- **Technological Solutions**
  - Turning regulatory obstacles into opportunities is one of Musk's superpowers. He often finds solutions that meet or beat the regulations.
    - **Starship Reusability**
      SpaceX's Starship solves the environmental and cost problems of traditional space exploration. By making rockets reusable, Musk has reduced the environmental impact of launches and met the regulatory requirement for sustainability (Space.com, 2023).

- **Battery Recycling Programs**
  Tesla has a comprehensive battery recycling program to meet environmental regulations and reduce waste. This is not only compliance but also Tesla's commitment to sustainability.

Musk's approach to regulatory hurdles—diplomacy, public engagement, and technology—sets the standard for navigating complex policy environments. By aligning his projects with regulatory goals, he is not only compliant but also advancing global sustainability and innovation. Through this, he is shaping renewable energy policy and regulatory frameworks and a collaborative and sustainable future for all.

Unite the World Through Innovation

Musk sees a future where countries work together on shared problems like space exploration, climate change, and sustainable energy. His companies, from Tesla's renewable energy solutions to SpaceX's interplanetary missions, show how technological advancements can unite governments, businesses, and individuals towards a common goal. That's how innovation crosses borders and creates global partnerships.

Musk's big ideas and projects are a challenge to the next generation of leaders. By showing how technology can drive change, he's encouraging policymakers to think big and solutions-focused. From rethinking urban mobility with Tesla to redefining communication with Starlink, Musk's work shows how technological vision must be integrated into policy making.

Closing his keynote address at the 2024 Global Innovation Summit, Musk emphasized the importance of aligning technology with humanity's aspirations:

"The future is what we make it. Let's build a world where technology uplifts humanity and policies empower progress."

This vision encapsulates Musk's belief in the transformative power of innovation, inspiring leaders, and citizens alike to collaborate in shaping a brighter, more sustainable future.

Balancing Work and Personal Life

Elon Musk—entrepreneur, engineer, futurist—is also a dad of eleven and values family life deeply. Despite running companies like Tesla, SpaceX, Neuralink and The Boring Company, he tries to have a real relationship with his kids and blend his intense work ethic with personal moments.

Family and Fatherhood

Musk's approach to family life is like him: honest, ambitious, and practical. He's often spoken about the importance of spending time with his kids, even in the midst of a crazy schedule. "I'm a pretty good dad," he said. "I make an effort to be there for the important moments" (Vance, 2017).

Musk has six kids from his first marriage to Canadian author Justine Wilson: Nevada Alexander (who passed away as an infant), twins Griffin and Xavier (who has transitioned and is now Vivian) and triplets Kai, Saxon, and Damian. He has three with musician Grimes: X Æ A-12 and twins Strider and Azure (Musk, 2023). In 2023, it was announced he also has a child with Neuralink executive Shivon Zilis (Fortune, 2023). They also welcomed another child at the beginning of 2024, but the name and gender weren't revealed. Each child, according to Musk, is raised with a focus on curiosity, learning and independence—things Musk values deeply (Vance, 2017).

A Balancing Act

Musk's work ethic is legendary. He works 80 to 100 hours a week, splits his time between companies and takes on projects that push the limits of human capability. Yet he makes time for his kids. "I'm with them as much as possible and make sure they feel loved," he's said in interviews (Vance, 2017).

Musk has been honest about how hard it is for him to balance his work goals with his personal responsibilities. "There are times I feel I'm not spending enough time with my kids or that I'm not doing enough at work," he admitted (Fortune, 2023). But he thinks that teaching his kids to work hard and be curious will prepare them for a future that values creativity and toughness.

Finding balance between Musk's giant professional ambitions and personal life is an ongoing challenge. He admits his career takes up most of his time and energy, but he's determined to find time with family. His philosophy on this is pragmatic: "There's no perfect formula," he's said, but try to prioritize what matters most (Vance, 2017).

Despite his public persona as a driven, sometimes ruthless innovator, his personal life shows a very human side. His relationship with his kids, his comments on parenting and his ongoing effort to balance work and family give us a better understanding of the man behind the innovations. His journey as a dad proves his point that success isn't just about professional achievements but about the legacy one leaves behind—both in advancing human progress and raising the next generation.

Musk's Perspective on Family and Legacy

Family is a big part of Musk's view of legacy. "Raising kids is one of the most important things anyone can do," he's said, and to inspire the next generation to think big and tackle the problems of humanity (Vance, 2017). While his public life gets all the attention, those around him say he's a devoted dad. For Musk, raising kids isn't just about their happiness but about giving them the tools to live meaningful, impactful lives.

Musk's approach to thinking extends to his parenting style. He's talked about fostering creativity and critical thinking in his kids, often in unconventional ways. "I want them to learn to think for themselves," he's said, because he believes education should ignite passion and curiosity, not conform to standards.

Personal Life Controversies and Challenges

Despite all the family values talk, Musk's personal life is complicated.

The Vivian Wilson Controversy

Elon Musk's relationship with his transgender daughter Vivian Jenna Wilson is a sore subject and a total contrast to his public image.

The estrangement is reportedly due to ideological and personal differences. Vivian distanced herself from Musk after she came out as transgender. According to reports, Musk called his daughter "dead to him" (NBC News, 2023). This has sparked a lot of backlash (NBC News, 2023). Unfortunately, Vivian wasn't able to receive acceptance from her father.

Musk blames "woke culture" for the rift between him and Vivian, saying in interviews that the influence of progressive ideas on young people has contributed to their estrangement (Financial Times, 2022). Critics say his comments are a deflection and contribute to the narrative around gender identity.

Criticism of Musk's Actions

Musk's parenting philosophy is all about independence and creativity, which he's talked about publicly many times. But many have pointed out the hypocrisy in his reaction to Vivian's transition. Advocacy groups have slammed Musk's stance, saying his behavior is not acceptable and perpetuates harmful transphobic stereotypes.

For example, LGBTQ+ advocacy groups like GLAAD have called out Musk's actions and words as problematic, saying we need influential people to model inclusivity and empathy.

Public vs. Private Persona

The controversy highlights the gap between Musk's public image as a visionary and hands-on dad and the reality of his private life.

- **Reputation:** While Musk is a tech and sustainability rockstar, this personal controversy has people questioning his values and ability to lead by example.
- **Bigger Picture:** This goes beyond Musk's family, it's about acceptance, empathy and identity. As one of the most visible people on the planet, Musk's actions set the tone for the public discourse on these issues.

Reflection on Leadership and Legacy

This raises big questions about the role of public figures in creating understanding and inclusivity. While Musk's work is transformative, his personal life is sparking debate about the intersection of personal values and public influence, especially as the owner of the biggest social media network.

The Vivian Wilson controversy is a reminder that leadership goes beyond professional accomplishments to include moral and interpersonal responsibilities. Time will tell if Musk can reconcile these parts of his life, but this is fuelling the conversation around authenticity, empathy, and the role of influential people.

A Creative Approach to Naming

Musk's kids' names show his unconventional thinking and futuristic vibes.

Nevada Alexander Musk: Musk's first child with his first wife Justine Wilson had a traditional name. **Sadly,** Nevada passed away at 10 weeks old from Sudden Infant Death Syndrome (SIDS) which Musk hardly ever talks about.

X Æ A-12 and Beyond: Musk's later kids' names went off the charts. His son with Grimes, X Æ A-12, became a meme for its weirdness.

Grimes explained the name as:

- X: The unknown variable, a math and science reference.
- Æ: Pronounced "Ash," artificial intelligence.

- A-12: Archangel-12, a reconnaissance plane known for its beauty and speed.

Despite the legal requirement for a simplified version of the name (X AE A-Xii), they kept the futuristic essence of it. This trend continued with their second kid, Exa Dark Sideræl Musk, aka Y, proving they're a match made in innovation heaven.

Hands-On Parenting

Musk has said he's a hands-on parent and spends time with his kids despite his crazy schedule. He does activities with them that align with his interests, like building model rockets, coding and exploring new tech. According to Ashlee Vance's biography, Musk once said his house could be a science lab as there are so many experiments and projects his kids are working on (Vance, 2017). These moments are not only educational but also helps him bond with them.

Education Pioneer

Musk was unhappy with the traditional school system so he co-founded Ad Astra, a private school that reflects his vision of education.

Innovative Features:

- **No Grades or Grade Levels:** No rigid grade levels so students' progress is based on what they know, not their age.
- **Problem-Solving Focus:** Curriculum is focused on solving real world problems through collaboration and critical thinking.
- **Hands-On Learning:** Students do projects not rote memorization.
- **Broader Goals:** Musk wants an education system that prepares kids for a rapidly changing world. Ad Astra is his manifestation of teaching kids to question norms, think for themselves and innovate.

Encouraging Independence

Musk teaches his kids independence and resilience. He believes these are the keys to success in an uncertain world. For example, he encourages his kids to explore their interests without fear of failure, to be curious and adaptable. This is how he approaches his own career, taking risks and pushing boundaries (Vance, 2017).

Balancing Legacy and Reality

Elon Musk's family life is just as complicated as his work life. Equal parts dreamer and realist, navigating the journey of parenthood. On one hand, there is creativity, knowledge, and strength. On the other hand, there is controversy and a real relationship.

Musk's family life is a painful and difficult legacy as he keeps changing the world with his large-scale projects. It highlights the brilliance and flaws of a man driven to shape the future.

End of Chapter 5 - Deep Insights: Present Day: Politics and Family Life

Chapter 5 - Quotes from Musk

- ❖ "I'm not a fan of politics. I'm focused on solving problems that matter for humanity's future." – Forbes, 2021
- ❖ "Free speech is the bedrock of a functioning democracy, and Twitter is the digital town square where matters vital to the future of humanity are debated." – Twitter, 2022
- ❖ "AI is a global challenge, and solving it requires international cooperation." – Financial Times, 2023
- ❖ "The real cost of carbon must be reflected in the market to drive meaningful change." – UN Climate Change, 2021

Chapter 5 - Interesting Facts

- ❖ Musk's push for AI control came from his worries about how technology could be abused. In 2014, at an MIT symposium, he said that AI was like "summoning the demon."
- ❖ He has proposed an "AI Safety Act," a framework for international cooperation on artificial intelligence governance, although it remains an idea rather than a formal policy.
- ❖ Musk's influence on renewable energy policies led to Tesla's large-scale battery projects, like the Hornsdale Power Reserve in Australia, which set global benchmarks for energy storage.
- ❖ Musk is a tech entrepreneur, but he often uses his platforms to ask governments to put climate policies, especially pricing carbon, at the top of their lists. He has said that this is necessary for sustainable energy.

Chapter 5 - Key Points

- ❖ **Pragmatic Politics:** Musk prioritizes practical solutions over ideological alignment, focusing on global challenges like climate change, space exploration, and AI safety.
- ❖ **Impact Through Innovation:** His ventures in renewable energy, autonomous transportation, and AI development are reshaping public policy and global sustainability efforts.
- ❖ **Leadership in Regulation:** Musk's proactive approach to AI governance emphasizes collaboration between governments, academia, and industry to mitigate risks while driving innovation.

Chapter 5 - Questions to Ponder

1. How does Musk's approach to politics differ from traditional politicians, and what can be learned from his focus on problem-solving?
2. In what ways has Musk's advocacy for AI regulation influenced global conversations about technology and ethics?
3. How do Musk's initiatives in renewable energy and space exploration demonstrate the intersection of technology and policy?

Chapter 5 - Activities

1. **Global Problem-Solving Activity:** Choose an immediate worldwide concern, such as AI regulation or climate change. Write a brief strategy detailing innovative solutions motivated by Musk's practical approach to problem-solving.
2. **Ethics in Technology Discussion:** Write a brief article or lead a conversation about the ethical consequences of artificial intelligence (AI) and how proactive regulation might influence its development.
3. **Carbon Impact Analysis:** Research carbon pricing and its effectiveness in combating climate change. Create a

presentation proposing how Musk's advocacy for carbon pricing could be implemented in your country.

Elon Musk: A Deeper Dive into Political Challenges and Collaborations

Elon Musk is more than a tech entrepreneur; he's a global figure whose work goes beyond business into politics, policy and governance. As founder of Tesla, SpaceX, Neuralink and other companies, he's disrupting industries and pushing the boundaries of what's possible for private companies. As his influence grows, so does the need to navigate the complexities of politics and government.

Musk's involvement in politics isn't about aligning with traditional ideologies, but about solving problems that matter for humanity's future. Whether it's carbon pricing, space policy, or global cooperation on AI safety, Musk sees politics as a means to an end: a way to make progress.

In this special chapter, we'll do a deeper examination of Musk's rising influence on global policy, his struggles to balance innovation and regulation, and their effects on his firms. We'll examine Musk's unconventional leadership and future vision as he redefines private enterprise and public policy, and what entrepreneurs and governments can learn from him.

Through his words and actions, Musk reminds us that the future is not something we wait for – it's something we build. This chapter invites you to dive into the strategies, challenges, and implications of Musk's politics and consider what it might mean for the world in the years to come.

Political Challenges Musk Faces

1. **Navigating Regulatory Complexities**
   Musk's businesses are on the forefront of technology and often move faster than the rules and regulations can keep up. This makes both problems and opportunities:
   - **SpaceX and Environmental Reviews:** The Federal Aviation Administration's (FAA) long reviews have caused the Starship program to be pushed

back more than once. Musk has complained about the slow pace, tweeting, "We need to simplify regulations to keep up with the speed of innovation" (Twitter, 2022). But SpaceX has also shown it can be flexible, working with regulators to address environmental concerns near its Boca Chica launch site. This resulted in revised plans that balance innovation with conservation.

- **Tesla and International Markets:**
Tesla's global expansion is tied to local regulations. For example, the European Union's strict safety and emissions standards require Tesla to tailor its cars to comply. Musk has also faced challenges in China, Tesla's second-largest market, where government policies on data privacy and EV subsidies change frequently. Musk's ability to adapt Tesla to different regulatory environments shows he's a pragmatist when it comes to politics.

Navigating these complexities also puts him ahead in other markets where they aren't asking him to meet high demands (yet), and it also encourages those markets to set those high regulations.

2. **Balancing Free Speech and Content Moderation on X (Twitter)**
Musk was at odds with governments around the world over content control and spreading false information after he bought Twitter (now X). Musk wants very little control to protect free speech, but he knows that a global platform is hard to manage.

- **Tensions with the EU:**
Under the EU's Digital Services Act (DSA), social media platforms must remove illegal content and reduce harmful misinformation. X has been warned about noncompliance, so Musk must balance his free speech philosophy with the law.

- **Combatting Bots and Fake News:**
Musk's introduction of subscription-based verification (X Premium) is part of his plan to reduce bot activity

and incentivize transparency. Critics say this monetizes credibility, but Musk says it's a step towards accountability on the platform.

3. **Navigating Geopolitical Tensions**

   Musk's ventures often collide with global politics and require diplomacy:

   - **Starlink in Ukraine:**
   Starlink's deployment in Ukraine during the 2022 invasion showed its value in keeping the internet on during conflicts. Some military uses of Starlink were limited by Musk's choice, though. This made people wonder what role private companies play in geopolitics.

   - **SpaceX's Global Satellite Network:**
   As Starlink grows, it's running into countries that are concerned about sovereignty and surveillance. How well Musk can negotiate with governments will decide Starlink's role in closing the digital divide.

4. **Navigating Policies Regarding AI**
   AI is so new that many countries don't have policies or regulations in place for it yet, but they do have policies in place for privacy. The AI project on X, referred to as Grok, has been facing challenges in the US and EU.

   - In the US it has come under scrutiny for spreading election-related misinformation. Another issue is that while Grok is currently only available to paying premium members of X, the information generated by Grok is being shared to everyone, "exacerbating the potential impacts of misinformation" according to Social Media Today.

   - In the EU, the issue is a privacy policy issue – the unapproved use of user data to train Grok, in which X responded by creating a new opt-out for it, but it's toggled on by default and most users aren't aware that it's even an option, so they don't know that they're agreeing to share their data to train Grok (TechTimes, 2024).

5. **Balancing Ethics with Progress**

The FDA had several concerns with Neuralink – the device's battery, whether the device could migrate within the brain, and the safe removal of the device if needed. The US Securities and Exchange Commission (SEC) was also concerned about the large amount of amount of euthanization of primates that underwent medical trials prior to human trials.

- In September 2023, Wired did an investigation and posted an article stating that letters were sent to the SEC by a medical ethics group to ask the agency to investigate Musk's claims that monkeys who died during Neuralink trials were terminally ill and did not die because of Neuralink implants. They claim, based on veterinary records, that complications with the implant procedures led to their deaths.
- Also in the article, an interview with a former employee and public records showed that as many as a dozen of Neuralink's primate subjects suffered due to the implant.
- Musk claimed on X that the animals were already close to death prior to implantation, but the former employee claimed that wasn't true as the animals must go through a year's worth of training before they can become subjects and none of them were close to death. Wired also noted that the monkeys were young, not even adults yet.

Collaborations and Policy Influence

1. **Public-Private Partnerships for Sustainability**
   Musk's sustainability goes beyond Tesla's EVs, into broader renewable energy:
   - **Hornsdale Power Reserve in Australia:** In 2017, Musk built the world's largest lithium-ion battery in South Australia to provide backup power during

outages. He made the bet on Twitter and delivered in under 100 days. Hornsdale has since inspired similar projects around the world, proving private innovation can solve public infrastructure problems.

- **Carbon Capture Advocacy:** Musk's $100 million XPRIZE for carbon removal technologies shows he believes governments and private companies must work together to solve climate change.

2. **AI Safety and Ethics**
Musk's involvement with OpenAI and Neuralink means he's tackling the ethics of advanced tech:
   - **Global AI Regulation:** Musk often calls for international AI oversight, comparing it to nuclear proliferation agreements. In a 2023 panel: "We need an AI equivalent of the Geneva Convention, so technology serves humanity, not harms it."
   - **Neuralink and Medical Ethics:** Neuralink's brain-machine interface trials have raised questions about human augmentation and consent. Musk says that transparency and working with medical boards are the ways to navigate these ethics.

3. **Space Policy and Multilateral Cooperation**
Musk sees a future where space brings nations together, not apart. To do that, SpaceX works with governments, offering affordable launch services and advocating for frameworks:
   - **Interplanetary Governance:** Musk has proposed an international space council to manage resources on Mars and other celestial bodies. He says that's the only way to prevent conflict over extraterrestrial resources.

Future for Musk's Companies

- **Tesla:** Musk's policy influence means Tesla will be at the head of the pack in the renewable energy transition. Carbon pricing could make sustainable energy solutions more competitive.

- **SpaceX:** As countries rely more on SpaceX for satellite launches and defense initiatives, Musk's role in space policy will grow. Partnerships will accelerate Mars colonization efforts.

- **Neuralink:** Musk's focus on medical applications for Neuralink lines up with global healthcare innovation priorities. Getting government approval will be key to scaling.

- **X (formerly Twitter):** Musk's goal for X is to be a global "everything app" and that requires navigating financial services, privacy, and content moderation regulatory hurdles.

Elon Musk's Growing Role in Politics

Elon Musk's companies have always gone beyond the traditional boundaries of business and into areas of societal impact that require working with governments and policymakers. His ability to navigate the intersection of innovation, regulation and diplomacy has helped him in his growing role as someone who doesn't just influence industries but shapes how they interact with the world.

From carbon pricing and renewable energy to international cooperation in AI and space, Musk's actions show he's committed to solving humanity's biggest problems. His leadership in SpaceX's Mars colonization, Tesla's clean energy and Neuralink's medical applications shows a vision that goes beyond profit – one that believes innovation can actually change the world.

But it's not without its challenges. Musk's outspokenness and ambitiousness often get him into trouble, and he has to balance public criticism with regulatory requirements. Whether it's dealing with misinformation on X, negotiating environmental permits for SpaceX, or ensuring Neuralink meets ethical standards, the path ahead is full of obstacles that will test his resolve and flexibility.

The future of Musk's companies is tied to his ability to shape global policies and public-private partnerships. His vision for the future – where technology serves humanity's greater good – is great, but it will require navigating complex geopolitics, regulatory hurdles, and societal expectations.

Musk's journey shows us that leadership in the 21st century requires more than innovation – it requires working with the systems that shape the world. His story tells us to dream big, act big and think about how technology, governance and human ambition can work together to make a better future.

As he says, "The future is ours to build." And by doing so, he's inviting us all to join in.

End of Chapter 6 - A Deeper Dive into Political Challenges and Collaborations

Chapter 6 – Quotes from Musk

- ❖ "We need to ensure technology serves humanity, not the other way around." (World Government Summit, 2017)

- ❖ "Innovation moves fast; regulation needs to move faster." (Twitter, 2022)

- ❖ "The future of humanity depends on global cooperation—whether it's in space, AI, or energy." (MIT AeroAstro Centennial Symposium, 2014)

- ❖ "Mars is a safety valve for Earth; it's not just an adventure, it's a necessity." (International Astronautical Congress, 2016)

Chapter 6 - Interesting Facts

- ❖ **Early Engagement with Carbon Pricing:** Musk was advocating for carbon pricing as a market-based solution to climate change as far back as 2015 and was lobbying governments to adopt carbon taxes to reduce emissions (The Guardian, 2015).

- ❖ **Starlink's Role in Disaster Response:** Starlink was used in disaster zones, like after Hurricane Ian in Florida in 2022, where it provided internet access during recovery efforts (CNBC, 2022).

- ❖ **Behind-the-Scenes Advocacy:** Musk has informally advised multiple US administrations on renewable energy and space policy (Politico, 2021).

- ❖ **Push for AI Regulation Since 2015:** Musk has been warning about AI risks since his 2015 TED Talk and has been urging international regulation to address misuse since (TED, 2015).

Chapter 6 - Key Points

- ❖ **The intersection of Innovation and Governance:** Musk's ventures show how private enterprise can shape and change public policy, e.g., SpaceX's partnerships with NASA (NASA, 2020).

- ❖ **Navigating Political Complexities:** Musk's pragmatic approach to regulation is seen in Tesla's adjustments to meet EU emissions standards (Reuters, 2021).

- ❖ **Global Collaboration for a Better Future:** Musk's call for international AI oversight shows we need to act together (New York Times, 2023).

Chapter 6 - Questions to Ponder

1. How does Elon Musk's approach to regulation and politics differ from that of other tech founders?

2. What are the pros and cons of private companies like SpaceX and Neuralink being major players in geopolitics and public policy?

3. How will Musk's innovation vs. regulation balance shape the future of global governance?

Chapter 6 - Activities

1. **Case Study Analysis:** Analyze how Musk's handling of SpaceX's FAA regulatory challenges impacted the Starship program.

2. **Debate Simulation:** Organize a debate on Musk's role in regulating AI, using his comparison of AI to nuclear weapons and the need for international treaties.

3. **Policy Proposal Workshop:** Create a policy proposal for one of Musk's initiatives, e.g. carbon capture technology or interplanetary governance, using his $100M XPRIZE for carbon removal.

The Future

As Elon Musk continues to change the world with his crazy ideas, we still don't know what his end game is. From making humanity a multiplanetary species to what he's doing now, Musk has always been trying to solve the biggest problems in the world and beyond. And it's far from over, and his vision for the future is bigger than ever.

Achievements Realized

Musk has achieved milestones that many once deemed impossible:

- ✓ **SpaceX:** Revolutionized space travel with reusable rockets, dramatically reducing costs and getting NASA contracts for moon and Mars missions. SpaceX's Falcon 9 was the first orbital-class rocket to land and be reused successfully (NASA, 2021).

- ✓ **Tesla:** Led the electric vehicle revolution and proved sustainable energy can be cool. Tesla's Model S was the first electric car to win MotorTrend's "Car of the Year," and the Model 3 is one of the best-selling EVs in the world (Tesla, 2023).

- ✓ **Neuralink:** Working on merging the human brain with AI through a brain-computer interface. Neuralink's first experiments are to restore mobility to paralyzed people, and Musk says the long-term goal is to make humans smarter (Neuralink, 2022).

- ✓ **The Boring Company:** Showcased new urban transportation solutions like the Las Vegas Loop, and how tunnelling can reduce traffic and improve urban mobility (The Boring Company, 2023).

Beyond Technology: Redefining Industries

Musk has not only advanced tech but entire industries. SpaceX has got the world interested in space again and governments and private companies are investing in similar programs. Tesla has accelerated the adoption of clean energy and forced legacy auto to move away from internal combustion engines. Musk has shown you can be profitable and sustainable, and a new generation of entrepreneurs is taking on the world.

Goals Still in Progress

Elon has achieved many things, but he still has many goals to achieve, such as colonizing Mars so humanity doesn't go extinct, expanding renewable energy to combat climate change, and making humanity sustainable with Neuralink and the Hyperloop. He's always pushing the boundaries of innovation and redefining what's possible for humanity. He's not done yet.

Colonizing Mars

One of Musk's biggest goals is to colonize Mars. Musk has been talking about a self-sustaining human settlement on the Red Planet for years.

SpaceX's Starship program is a big step towards this vision. Starship can carry both people and cargo and has done multiple test flights and has shown it can go deep space.

They're preparing for the first crewed missions to the Red Planet and Musk is aiming for launch within the next 10 years. "This is not just about exploration—it's about survival," Musk explained, emphasizing the need for a multiplanetary existence to safeguard humanity (Musk, 2018).

But a thriving Martian settlement will require:

- **Radiation Exposure:** Astronauts going to Mars will be exposed to cosmic radiation for prolonged periods, so we need advanced shielding technologies.

- **Life Support Systems:** Sustainable habitats on Mars need closed-loop life support systems that can recycle air, water, and food.

- **Economic Feasibility**: Musk has said we need to reduce costs dramatically and a ticket to Mars must be affordable for millions to consider migration (SpaceX, 2023).

Despite these challenges Musk's Mars colonization has got the world interested in space again and governments and private companies are investing in interplanetary tech.

Solving Artificial General Intelligence (AGI) Challenges

Musk is tackling the AGI challenges in his work with Neuralink and his previous work with OpenAI. He sees a future where humans live alongside advanced AI, using its capabilities while mitigating the risks.

Neuralink is moving fast. In 2023, they started human trials, a big step towards treating brain conditions and augmenting human ability.

"This technology has the potential to restore abilities and create new ones we can't yet imagine," Musk stated during a Neuralink update (Neuralink, 2023). Initial applications include:

- Restore mobility for people with paralysis.

- Cure Alzheimer's and Parkinson's.

- Bridge human cognition and AI to create new forms of human-AI collaboration.

Neuralink's brain-computer interfaces (BCIs) will bridge the gap between humans and machines. The initial focus is on medical applications, but Musk sees Neuralink as a tool for human augmentation so we can "keep up" with the rapidly advancing AI (Neuralink, 2022).

Yet, the pursuit of AGI comes with profound ethical dilemmas:

- **Existential Risks:** Musk often warns of the risks of unregulated AI development and calls for global cooperation and strong oversight (Musk, 2017).
- **Alignment with Human Values:** Getting AGI to act in humanity's best interest is a problem that requires technologists, ethicists, and policymakers to work together.

Musk's dual approach—advancing AI tech while advocating for responsible innovation – shows he wants AGI to be a force for good.

Sustainable Energy for All

Tesla's mission to get the world to sustainable energy is a big part of Elon's vision. Beyond the electric vehicle (EV) market, Tesla wants to change how energy is produced, stored, and consumed globally. These efforts will create a carbon-neutral world by making clean energy available and scalable. The company is laying the groundwork for a global transition to sustainability, climate change and energy independence.

Key Initiatives

1. **Solar Power Solutions**
   Tesla's Solar Roof combines solar panels with roof tiles, giving homeowners a beautiful and efficient way to get renewable energy. This eliminates the need for traditional solar panels and fits into the design of the home, so more people can get clean energy (Tesla, 2023; Energy Sage, 2023).

2. **Energy Storage**
   The Megapack, Tesla's energy storage product, is for utility companies. It stabilizes the grid, stores energy for peak demand periods and reduces fossil fuels. It's been deployed in projects around the world and is showing how energy infrastructure can be transformed (Tesla, 2023; Bloomberg, 2023).

3. **AI-Driven Energy Management**
   Musk has mentioned using AI in energy systems to optimize

production, storage, and consumption. AI could do predictive analytics for grid management, real-time energy distribution and cost savings for consumers by reducing waste and maximizing efficiency (Tesla, 2023; MIT Technology Review, 2023).

AI in Energy Management

AI is changing the game for energy production and consumption. Musk wants AI to not only optimize individual energy use but grid-level management.

1. **Energy Optimization for Consumers:** Tesla's Powerwall and Powerpack systems with AI-driven software like Autobidder allow you to manage your energy use. These systems learn your consumption habits, predict demand, and make sure energy is available when you need it, reducing waste and cost.

2. **Grid-Level Solutions:** Tesla's Megapack projects are changing how utilities manage energy. With AI, these large-scale battery systems can stabilize the grid, balance supply and demand and prevent outages during peak usage.

3. **Smart Integration:** AI-driven platforms let renewable energy sources like solar and wind to be smoothly included into the current grid. This guarantees a constant and dependable power supply even in cases of changing natural energy sources.

A Carbon-Neutral Future

Tesla's approach is all part of Musk's vision for global energy independence and a carbon-neutral world. By having solutions for homes, businesses and utilities, Tesla is creating sustainable communities everywhere. This reduces greenhouse gas emissions and gives individuals and organizations control over their energy.

By reducing fossil fuels, increasing renewable energy, and making sustainable living global, Tesla is making clean energy the new normal.

Musk has said solving the energy crisis is one of his top priorities. "Our goal is to transition the world to sustainable energy as quickly as possible," Musk remarked during Tesla's 2023 shareholder meeting. These advancements represent not only technical progress but also a profound step toward a carbon-neutral world.

Next-Generation Batteries

Tesla is leading battery innovation, creating products that are more efficient, cost-effective, and environmentally friendly. This is key to accelerating EVs and renewable energy.

1. **Longer Lifespans and Higher Densities:** Tesla's new battery chemistries, like LFP and silicon-based anodes, will have longer durability and more energy storage, so EVs can go further on a single charge and renewable energy systems can store more power.

2. **Cost Reduction:** The 4680 cell is designed to reduce production cost by 56% while increasing performance. According to Tesla, this will be the cost per kilowatt hour.

3. **Recycling Initiatives:** Tesla is recycling batteries to recover lithium, cobalt, and nickel. A closed loop.

Pioneering Community Solutions

Tesla's commitment to sustainability extends beyond individual goods to community-based solutions. Tesla is leading the charge on community projects that make entire communities energy independent.

- **Solar Neighborhoods:** Tesla is building communities powered by its Solar Roofs and Powerwalls, like the SunHouse at Easton Park in Austin, Texas. These neighborhoods show

that living off-grid is possible with sustainable energy solutions.
- **Global Projects:** Tesla's utility-scale energy storage projects like Hornsdale Power Reserve in Australia.

Transforming X into the "Everything App"

Elon Musk's buying and rebranding of Twitter into X is a big step towards his vision of a global "everything app." This app will combine communication, commerce, and AI services into one digital ecosystem and change how we interact online.

Features in Progress

1. **Payments Integration**
   Musk has announced payments will be added, peer-to-peer transactions, online shopping and financial services will be available within the app. This will make X a one-stop shop for personal and business financial needs (Musk, 2023; X Corp, 2023)

2. **AI-Driven Personalization**
   X is using advanced algorithms to deliver more personalized content and services. This includes recommendations for entertainment, education, and professional tools to increase user engagement and utility (X Corp., 2023; The Verge, 2023).

3. **Creative Economy**
   With a focus on creators, X is adding content publishing, monetization, and audience engagement tools. This will make the platform a home for creators and entrepreneurs and a thriving ecosystem of innovation and expression (Musk, 2023; X Corp, 2023)

X's success will depend on user adoption and being a single cohesive experience. While it's a work in progress, Musk's iterative approach and constant innovation shows he's committed to changing the way we interact online. X's journey is not just about a platform but about the broader shift in the digital world where ecosystems, not apps, will be the future (Musk, 2023; Business Insider, 2023)

Balancing Ambition and Legacy

For Musk, success is not just about technology; it's about leaving a good legacy for humanity. "I want to be able to look back and say I did everything I could to make life better for as many people as possible," he said in an interview (Musk, 2015). This is what drives his many ambitious projects across many industries, from accelerating renewable energy to making life multi-planetary through space exploration.

However, he must sacrifice much to achieve his goals. Musk has admitted that stress and pressure are to blame for his inability to balance work and family Because he thinks it will help make the world a better place in the future, he is motivated to finish his job no matter what.

Musk also wants to inspire the next generation, including his own kids. He envisions a world transformed by his innovations – a world where sustainable energy, space colonization and cool technologies are the new normal. By pursuing his bold vision, he wants to create opportunities for the next generation to thrive and build upon what he's building. Whether through Tesla, SpaceX or other companies, Musk's ultimate goal is to leave behind a legacy of progress, innovation, and hope for a better tomorrow.

The Final Frontier

Elon Musk's story is not over yet. Whether it's space exploration with SpaceX, making life multi-planetary, understanding human cognition with Neuralink, or revolutionizing energy and electric cars with Tesla, his vision goes far beyond today. His work doesn't stop there – Musk is also working on global internet with Starlink and rethinking transportation with the Boring Company's tunnel systems.

Musk's story is a testament to the power of passion, resilience, and the ability to turn dreams into reality. From failing with the first SpaceX rocket launches to scaling Tesla's production, his persistence has been key to his success. His work shows us that no goal is too big, no challenge too hard and no future is unachievable when you have a vision for a better world. Musk's legacy will continue to inspire us and show us what's possible with human imagination and determination.

End of Chapter 7 – Deep Insight: The Future

Chapter 7 - Quotes from Musk

- "This is not just about exploration—it's about survival. Humanity must become a multiplanetary species to safeguard its future." – Musk at the 2018 International Astronautical Congress.
- "AI could be humanity's greatest invention or its biggest existential threat. It's up to us to decide." – Financial Times, 2017
- "Our goal is to transition the world to sustainable energy as quickly as possible. We don't have time to wait." – Tesla Shareholder Meeting, 2023
- "I want to look back and know I did everything possible to make life better for as many people as I could." – Rolling Stone, 2015

Chapter 7 - Interesting Facts

- He named his first reusable rocket project Grasshopper because it could "hop" during test flights, which is where the idea for SpaceX's reusable Falcon rockets came from.
- Neuralink's early testing is focused on giving mobility to paralyzed people by linking brain signals to computers, with the long-term goal of telepathic communication.
- Tesla's Gigafactories will be 100% renewable energy powered, with on-site solar and wind farms in the future.
- He's also been working on "carbon capture farms" to physically remove CO_2 from the air, not as well-known a part of his sustainability efforts.

Chapter 7 - Key Points

- ❖ **Space Pioneering:** SpaceX is working towards a permanent human settlement on Mars, making humanity a multiplanetary species and reducing existential risks.
- ❖ **Sustainability:** Tesla and his renewable energy projects are getting the world to carbon neutral through solar, battery and energy storage.
- ❖ **Ethics and Tech:** Through Neuralink and his AI governance advocacy, Musk is testing the limits of tech while emphasizing the importance of ethics.

Chapter 7 – Questions to Ponder

1. How does Mars colonization fit into Musk's overall plan for humanity's survival?
2. What are the biggest challenges in balancing tech with ethics, especially with AI and Neuralink?
3. How has Musk's ability to do multiple industries have inspired or challenged your own entrepreneurial and problem solving?

Chapter 7 – Activities

1. **Moonshot Thinking Exercise:** Choose a global problem (e.g., climate change or energy scarcity). Brainstorm bold, Musk-like solutions, how would you solve it with current technology.
2. **Sustainability Audit:** Audit your own energy usage and identify areas where you can be more sustainable, inspired by Musk's renewable energy projects. Create a plan to implement those changes in your daily life.
3. **AI Ethics Debate:** Research current AI developments and organize a discussion on their risks and benefits. Propose guidelines for responsible innovation that address some of Musk's AGI concerns.

Timeline of Elon Musk's Life

1971
- Born on June 28 in Pretoria, South Africa, to Errol Musk and Maye Musk.

1981
- At age 10, develops an interest in computers and learns programming. Creates and sells his first software game, *Blastar*, by age 12.

1989
- Moves to Canada to attend Queen's University and avoid mandatory military service in South Africa.

1992
- Transfers to the University of Pennsylvania, earning degrees in Physics and Economics.

1995
- Enrolls in a PhD program at Stanford but drops out after two days to pursue entrepreneurship. Co-founds Zip2, a city guide software company.

1999
- Compaq acquires Zip2 for $307 million. Musk earns $22 million from the sale.
- Co-founds X.com, an online payment company.

2000
- X.com merges with Confinity and becomes PayPal.

2002
- eBay acquires PayPal for $1.5 billion, earning Musk $165 million.

- Founds SpaceX (Space Exploration Technologies Corp.) to revolutionize space travel.

2004
- Invests in and becomes chairperson of Tesla Motors (later Tesla, Inc.), aiming to advance electric vehicles.

2008
- Tesla releases its first car, the Tesla Roadster.
- SpaceX successfully launches its first rocket, Falcon 1, into orbit.

2010
- Tesla goes public, becoming the first American car company to do so since Ford in 1956.

2012
- SpaceX's Dragon spacecraft becomes the first commercial spacecraft to dock with the International Space Station (ISS).

2015
- Co-founds OpenAI to promote and develop friendly AI for humanity.

2016
- Founds Neuralink to develop brain-machine interface technology.
- Founds The Boring Company to build tunnels for transportation and infrastructure solutions.

2018
- Tesla launches the Model 3, its first mass-market electric vehicle.
- SpaceX successfully launches the Falcon Heavy, the most powerful operational rocket in the world.

2020
- SpaceX's Crew Dragon spacecraft completes its first crewed mission, marking NASA's return to launching astronauts from U.S. soil.

2022
- Completes the $44 billion acquisition of Twitter, rebranding it to X and envisioning it as an "everything app."

Present
- Continues to lead SpaceX, Tesla, Neuralink, X, and The Boring Company while championing sustainability, innovation, and the future of humanity through ambitious ventures on Earth and beyond.

Trivia Questions

1. What country was Elon Musk born in?
2. At what age did Elon Musk create and sell his first video game, *Blastar*?
3. Which university did Elon Musk first attend when he moved to Canada?
4. What degrees did Musk earn at the University of Pennsylvania?
5. What was the name of the first company Elon Musk co-founded?
6. How much did Compaq pay to acquire Zip2?
7. What was X.com, the company Musk co-founded in 1999, best known for?
8. How much did Elon Musk make from the sale of PayPal to eBay?
9. In what year did Elon Musk found SpaceX?
10. What was the name of SpaceX's first rocket to successfully reach orbit?
11. What was Tesla's first electric vehicle?
12. Which Tesla model is considered the company's first mass-market electric car?
13. What is the goal of Neuralink, the company Musk founded in 2016?
14. What does The Boring Company primarily focus on?
15. What AI research organization did Musk co-found in 2015?
16. How many children does Elon Musk have?
17. What is the name of Musk's first child with singer Grimes?
18. What inspired Musk's interest in space exploration as a child?

19. In what year did Musk acquire Twitter?

20. What is Musk's vision for X (formerly Twitter)?

Answers to Trivia Questions

1. South Africa
2. 12
3. Queen's University
4. Physics and Economics
5. Zip2
6. $307 million
7. Online payments; later became PayPal
8. $165 million
9. 2002
10. Falcon 1
11. Tesla Roadster
12. Model 3
13. Developing brain-machine interface technology
14. Tunnelling and infrastructure for transportation
15. OpenAI
16. 11
17. X Æ A-12 Musk
18. Reading science fiction books and comics
19. 2022
20. Transforming it into an "everything app" similar to WeChat

Discussion Questions

1. How did his early interest in tech and reading lead to his career?
2. How did growing up in South Africa shape his worldview and goals?
3. How big of an impact was moving to North America for education and career?
4. What did he learn from Zip2 and PayPal that he applied to later companies?
5. How was X.com different from what PayPal became?
6. How big of an impact did his early financial success have in allowing him to take risks with SpaceX and Tesla?
7. What made him want to go into private space with SpaceX?
8. How has Tesla changed the public perception and adoption of electric cars?
9. What's been the most important innovation from SpaceX? Why?
10. How does Neuralink fit into his long-term vision for humanity?
11. What role will The Boring Company play in solving urban infrastructure?
12. Does his involvement in multiple industries help or hurt his ability to achieve his goals?
13. How have his personal struggles shaped his business and leadership approach?
14. He's been open about his work ethic and long hours. How does that impact his personal relationships and overall health?
15. How does he balance being a dad with his crazy professional life?

16. What do you think about him buying Twitter (now X)?

17. How likely is he to turn X into an "everything app"?

18. How has his approach to content moderation on X changed the conversation around free speech and online safety?

19. He often says you should take risks and go big. Do you agree?

20. How do his companies reflect his long-term view of humanity's existence and progress?

21. How will his achievements impact future innovators and entrepreneurs?

Thank you so much for reading!

If you enjoyed this book, we'd love to hear your thoughts! Leaving a review on Amazon is a wonderful way to give the book a thumbs-up and help other readers discover it. It only takes a minute—simply scan the QR code to get started.

We truly appreciate your support and your feedback—thank you for helping others find this story!

William Isaac

Made in United States
North Haven, CT
24 February 2025